CRACKING THE LOVE CODE

Cracking the Love Code

♥ ♥ ♥ ♥ ♥ ♥ ♥ ♥ ♥ ♡ ♥ ♥ ♥ ♥

Six Proven Principles to Find and Keep Real Love with the Right Person

JANET O'NEAL

"The Love Coach"

BROADWAY BOOKS

New York

A hardcover edition of this book was published in 1998 by Broadway Books.

Broadway Books titles may be purchased for business or promotional use or for special sales. For information, please write to: Special Markets Department, Random House, Inc., 1540 Broadway, New York, NY 10036.

BROADWAY BOOKS and its logo, a letter B bisected on the diagonal, are trademarks of Broadway Books, a division of Random House, Inc.

First trade paperback edition published 1999.

Designed by Susan Hood

The Library of Congress has catalogued the hardcover edition as:
O'Neal, Janet.
Cracking the love code : six proven principles to find and keep real love with the right person / by Janet O'Neal.
p. cm.
Originally published: Houston, Tex. : Wolf & Madison, 1996.
Includes bibliographical references.
ISBN 0-7679-0167-3 (hc)
1. Mate selection. 2. Man-woman relationships. I. Title.
HQ801.052 1998
646.7'7—dc21 97-28081
CIP

ISBN 0-7679-0168-1

TO MY FAMILY:

BOTH BY BLOOD AND BY CHOICE

Contents

Acknowledgments ix

Introduction 1

The First Principle: Conceiving 11
Determining what you want in a relationship (and what you have to offer somebody else); setting your goals for happiness.

The Second Principle: Contentment 47
The top needs of women and men in a relationship; how to get all of your needs met while meeting all the needs of the other person.

The Third Principle: Connecting 73
Learning to make a link or a bond with another person in order to set the groundwork for a real relationship (as opposed to a flirtation or a one-night stand).

The Fourth Principle: Chemistry 119
In a word, SEX. Understanding men's and women's top sexual turn-ons and turn-offs, plus an honest look at safe-sex issues.

The Fifth Principle: Conviction 159
The bewildering but wonderful process of becoming convinced that your partner is the right person for you.

The Sixth Principle: Commitment 193
The big "C": Deciding whether or not to make a commitment to your partner.

Write to the Author 229

Acknowledgments

Many people helped in the creation of this book.
I wish especially to thank:

The thousands of men and women I've worked with over the years,
whose trials and successes helped me
"crack the love code"

Dr. Bob and Dr. Leah Schwartz,
for your unconditional love,
faith, and support

Nancy Neill,
for your friendship, your wit,
and your no-nonsense advice

Joe Vitale,
my book coach

Jim Evans,
for your moral support and
adept guidance through the
"birthing" process of this book

Dave Rice,
for always being there
year after year

Dan Sessions,
for your calmness
and your audio expertise

Kim Widacki,
for superb transcribing

Dorothy, Jeannie, and Carol,
who have become my guardian
angels of deadline management

Hazel Crowe,
my mother,
who has always believed in me

Ray Meader,
my father,
who taught me to love books

Robert Meader,
my brother,
whose love I can always
count on

Jane Dystel,
my wonderful literary agent,
and her superb staff

Lauren Marino,
my savvy editor,
and everyone at
Broadway Books

Robert A. Knowlton,
for your encouragement, advice,
and support

Moose,
for contributions too numerous
to mention

Ron Kaye,
the "Anti-diplomat"

Connie Schmidt,
my original editor,
who helped me turn this into
a book I'm proud of !

Kati Steele,
for her persistence
and enthusiasm

And to God,
who has never given me more than I can handle

Introduction

LOVE COACH CRACKS LOVE CODE . . . AND A BOOK IS BORN

One recent morning I was in my office when the phone rang. It was one of my clients, Mary Ann, letting me know that after working with me on her commitment problems, she and her fiancé Jim were to be married September 8. She thanked me, not just for introducing her and Jim but for helping them work through commitment issues that would otherwise have torn their relationship apart. "You're invited to the wedding, of course," she said.

I hung up with a big grin on my face.

The phone rang again. This time it was Harold, another client. He was ecstatic because, thanks to my coaching him for a few weeks, he had been able to get past the fourth month in his latest relationship. Before, his relationships had always crumbled after a couple of months, because Harold didn't know how to navigate "the switch." The switch is a bewildering but common phenomenon in which the person who was the pursuer becomes the pursued, and vice versa. This can be a true crisis point in a relationship; I discuss it in detail in chapter five, "Conviction." "Getting past the switch was a real accomplishment for me," Harold said. "You know, I think this is the woman I'm going to marry."

No sooner had I hung up from Harold than the phone rang once again—and I could see it was going to be another typical morning at Friend Connection. It was Nancy on the line, telling me that she had refused to go to bed with somebody she'd been dating for a short time, and she'd based her decision on the check-list I had given her two weeks before. The man had not taken her refusal with good grace. "He got very angry," she told me, "which only confirmed in my mind that he had no real feelings for me." After she had broken off with this man, she had accepted a date with a very good-looking young lawyer. They'd already been out three times, and she felt he might really be "the one." "In the past," Nancy said, "I would have never been available to even meet this man; I would have been too busy having meaningless sex with a man who was probably a promiscuous, inconsiderate jerk." I congratulated her on her accomplishment and wished her luck.

After a few more phone conversations I asked the receptionist to hold my calls, because something had been gnawing at me all morning. Actually it had been bothering me for some time, but the feeling was becoming more persistent, and I needed time to reflect.

For over a decade I'd been running Friend Connection, the most successful independent video dating service in the United States. People called me every day to thank me and my staff for helping them find happiness. Some of them—couples and individuals alike—were calling me and offering me eye-popping amounts of money to counsel them. My business was a huge success. I was living the American Dream, and helping others live their dreams, too.

So . . . why wasn't I feeling totally satisfied?

I reflected some more. In the years I had owned Friend Connection I had worked with thousands of members. I was 100 percent dedicated to improving the quality of people's relationships by helping them find a better way to connect with others. I'd helped countless couples meet and marry, and many of them later introduced me to the children that resulted from their union. It made me feel so wonderful to see those children and to know that I was helping bring joy to my clients.

I had also worked one-on-one with many people, helping them

with their relationship challenges and steadily earning a reputation as "The Love Coach."

In addition to all this, I had done numerous surveys that I felt truly probed the hearts, minds, and souls of men and women. The questions covered everything from turn-ons and turn-offs on dates to the truth about sexual conduct in the nineties. The surveys were taken in segments of five hundred people at a time, some with the assistance of Rice University graduate students. Respondents ranged in age from the early twenties through the early fifties.

It wasn't long before a pattern had begun to emerge, and as it did, two points became clear to me:

1. The same issues kept coming up over and over again for couples, depending upon how long they had been dating ("the switch" being one troubling example). Relationships, I discovered, are characterized by distinct stages, and each stage presents its own set of challenges.
2. Even more important, *the people who were successful in their unions brought certain relationship skills with them to the table before they even began dating their partner.* As I continued with my surveys and my work with my clients, I gained a clearer picture of the difference between people who were able to attract successful unions and others who "failed" over and over.

I had begun to realize there was actually a formula to finding a happy, successful relationship.

As I learned more about what this formula was (which I'll explain in just a few moments), it became equally clear to me what it *wasn't*. It wasn't some profound mystery. It wasn't about playing by some set of old-fashioned, intimacy-prohibiting rules that made the opposite sex a "prize" to be won, nor was it about treating the opposite sex as if they were so drastically different from you that they came from another universe.

After all my years of coaching and counseling and studying, I believed I really knew what worked and what didn't in relationships. I felt I had it down to a science as well as an art.

I felt I had actually cracked the "Love Code."

So why wasn't I satisfied? Why was I sometimes so profoundly frustrated? What was missing?

And then it hit me, and I knew the reason for my discontent. In spite of all the people I was helping, I was still haunted by all those I hadn't been able to assist. I was only one person, after all, and could only do so much. There had to be a way to reach more people.

Then and there I knew it was time to sell Friend Connection. This was accomplished in less than two months, and I took the next twelve months off to begin working on my dream: writing a book that would make my formula for happy relationships accessible to everybody.

The project quickly became an obsession. Not only did I experience that common feeling people have when they realize they have a book in them—I absolutely felt that the book weighed on me like a ten-month pregnancy. I knew I would be paralyzed until I "gave birth" to this book.

In short, I felt compelled to get my message out.

I began by writing down the basics about my formula, trying to package it in such a way that it would be easy to remember. I didn't want readers to have to waste time struggling to recall, "Now, what was that second principle again?" I'd seen too many self-help books where the message was lost in a bewildering array of steps or secrets or rules.

I finally hit upon the "C" Formula—six profoundly important principles to building a happy, lasting relationship. Countless testimonials from users let me know my "C" Formula program really worked.

For example, Susan wrote to me that the "critical flaws" checklist I had given her probably saved her from making one of the most disastrous mistakes of her life. "Thanks to that list," she wrote, "I was able to avoid a man who almost surely would have brought me years of grief. Now I'm in a relationship that looks like it may be *the* one." (You'll find the "critical flaws" list in chapter three, "Connecting.")

Then there was Rachel, who had not had a date in nearly two

years. "You can imagine what my self-esteem level was like," she told me. "I began working with the personal asset inventory and the 'wish-list' exercises you gave me. Doing those exercises really did give me the confidence to go out there again, with a much clearer idea of who I am and what I'm looking for in a relationship. I know I'll eventually settle down and get married to the right person for me, but for now I'm dating three great men and having the time of my life." If it worked for Rachel, it will work for you; you'll find the exercises she was talking about in chapter one, "Conceiving."

My files are full of similar testimonials. The bottom line is, I wrote *Cracking the Love Code* because I have seen so many real-life successes resulting from my formula, and it is my strong desire that *everybody* benefit from my years of research in the field. This book takes the results of all of my research—all the mistakes and successes of my thousands of clients—and puts it one place.

Every person has the potential to develop the basic skills necessary for finding—and keeping—real love with the right person. It is my fondest wish that everybody develop those skills. At the risk of sounding like a Miss America contestant, I truly have a vision of a happier, more loving world, and I like to think I'm doing my part to make that come to pass.

SO WHAT CAN THIS BOOK DO FOR YOU?

Cracking the Love Code can change your life for the better. If you read it carefully and do all of the exercises, I guarantee it will improve your relationships. Most important, it's going to help you get what you want—whether you want to get married to your soul mate or merely begin dating and having an active personal life. In fact, this book can even help you if you're already *in* a relationship and want to make it better than you might have imagined was possible. There are only a few requirements:

1. *Get very clear on what you want.*
2. *Take action.*
3. *Follow the plan in the book.*

THE "C" FORMULA EXPLAINED

I have divided this book into six chapters, with each chapter covering one key principle about relationships. These six principles correspond roughly to the relationship stages I mentioned earlier. To make it all easy to remember, each principle is a word that begins with the letter C. Here, then, are the six principles that constitute the "Love Code":

1. ***Conceiving:*** Discovering how to form a clear and complete "wish list" of everything you want in your mate—characteristics, interests, attitudes. Determining what you want in a relationship (and, equally important, what you have to offer somebody else). Setting your goals for happiness. Includes visualization techniques that will easily and naturally lead you to the right partner. Without this work, you will risk attracting the same wrong person over and over again.
2. ***Contentment:*** Learning how to truly satisfy your partner while ensuring your own needs are met. Includes an eye-opening list of the top seven emotional needs of a man, and the seven *different* needs of a woman. If these rudimentary needs are not met for both of you, the relationship cannot be successful. Furthermore, you must have the skills to meet the needs of the opposite sex before you even *begin* a relationship.
3. ***Connecting:*** Discovering how to truly connect with another person in order to set the groundwork for a *real* relationship—as opposed to a flirtation or a one-night stand. Includes eleven secrets for establishing rapport with the opposite sex, as well as a "critical flaws" checklist to help you avoid getting involved with someone who can never bring you happiness. After you master these skills, you will know you can *always* attract another relationship.
4. ***Chemistry:*** In a word, SEX. Understanding men's and women's top sexual turn-ons and turn-offs, plus an honest look at safe-sex issues. Includes a list of questions you and your part-

ner need to ask yourselves while you still have your clothes on. Read this to have toe-curling sex with the right person. Don't just desire a great lover; *be* one!

5. ***Conviction:*** The bewildering but wonderful process of becoming convinced that your partner is the right person for you. Includes detailed and tested guidelines for compatibility, plus tips on how to find the weak points in a relationship—and how to fix them. Don't wonder whether someone is right for you; *know*.
6. ***Commitment:*** The big "C": deciding whether or not to make a lifelong commitment to your partner. Includes the eleven fears that keep people from taking this big step—and how to handle them. Shows how to avoid making a pledge to the wrong person—or letting the right person get away. This chapter will help you make what could very well be the single most important decision of your life.

MAKING THE LOVE CODE WORK FOR YOU

Now that you know the six principles, here are two points that will make this system really work for you:

1. Begin at the beginning of the book. Read through the chapters and study the principles in the order in which they're presented. Do this even if you're *in* a relationship.
2. Do the exercises. You may think exercises are superfluous, but they are there for a reason. I'm sure you could breeze through this book and have an intellectual understanding of the principles—but these principles are not something you "get" merely on an intellectual level; they are something you *do* in your heart. The exercises are designed to help you clarify your wants and needs, and to help reinforce what you've learned. Doing them will help ensure you actually put the principles to work.

This entire book is designed to be interactive. It asks a lot of questions, because these are questions *you* need to be asking about the relationship. That's why it's so important that you really think about the questions and answer them honestly.

If you leave something out—if you skip a chapter or even an exercise—because you think it doesn't apply to you, you might end up throwing away a relationship that is actually good for you, or staying in one that's absolutely disastrous for you. Worse yet, you may actually end up married and not committed. That's not a contradiction in terms; sadly enough, it happens all the time. Life is too short to waste in a marriage where one or both people are not committed.

This brings me to another point I want to stress: unlike many other relationship books out there, this book makes it clear that ***marriage is not necessarily the goal.*** The goal is to decide what will make you happy, and then to go out and get it. However, if your idea of happiness *is* matrimony, then don't you want a happy, loving, mutually supportive union—one in which both of you *are* committed? Of course you do. That's another reason it's particularly important for you to work on all the steps in this book.

Maybe you still have doubts. Perhaps at this point you're still thinking, "Well, maybe this book will work for some people, but it's not going to work for me. I mean, I've been married five times!" Or, "There's no way this can work for me. I haven't had a date in two years." Or, "It's just not going to work for me. There isn't another person in the world who's really going to be compatible with someone like me."

There's no way I can lay all of your doubts to rest in the course of one brief introduction. But I can tell you this: it doesn't matter where you are now in your life, or where you have been. ***Your past does NOT have to equal your future.*** No matter what your past has been, you *can* change your life and create the loving, joyous relationship you've always wanted.

Wherever you are in your life is a "perfect" place for you right now. *Now* is the perfect time and place for you to start creating the relationship you want. I'm going to show you, step-by-step, how to create that relationship.

There are millions of people out there, and at least one of them is the right person for you. You just need the skills to go out and find that person, and that's what this book will teach you.

Or maybe you think you've already found the right person; reading this book can help you determine if this is so. Even if you're in an absolutely terrific relationship, applying these principles can make that union infinitely more fulfilling for you and your partner.

Enough of the preliminaries, then. Are you ready to embark on a journey that can change your life forever? Are you ready to finally start attracting the people and experiences that will make your life joyful? Are you ready to begin producing absolute magic in your life? Then turn the page, and let's get started.

♥ The First Principle ♥

CONCEIVING

Everything begins with knowing what you want. Before you can have anything in life—including a fulfilling relationship—you have to know exactly what you want. Many people seem to have a pretty clear idea of what they don't want, but starting out on such a negative note will not get you where you want to go. So we're going to start by creating a positive framework from which to build the life you desire.

One of my favorite movies is *Tombstone*. There's a scene in that movie where Doc Holliday, played by Val Kilmer, is dying. Wyatt Earp goes to him, very distraught, but instead of expressing compassion for Doc, Wyatt is preoccupied with his own troubles. He begins to talk about his problems: he's married and has four children, his wife is addicted to morphine and their relationship has fallen apart, and he has fallen in love with an actress and wants to travel the world with her. He tells Doc that all he really wants to do is be a "normal" person. Normal people, in his view, are married; they stay home and they're content. This view is what made him get married in the first place. But Wyatt has fallen madly in love with a woman who is not his wife but with whom he feels he wants to share his entire life. When he's with her, he feels he can do anything. "What do I do?" he asks Doc plaintively.

Doc tells Wyatt that life is like a poker game. We do not all get the same cards; we have to play the hand we're dealt. The cards we get are not as important as how we play them. Doc advises Wyatt that he must follow his own path and his own beliefs. He must find his joy in his own way.

Given that this is obviously a 1990s spin on an 1800s story, the point is well taken, nevertheless. Wyatt had a tough choice to make. He couldn't have his cake and eat it, too. In the end he did not settle for the traditional life of domestic bliss. While upholding his financial responsibility for his wife and children, he traveled the world for the next thirty years with the love of his life, and he was tremendously happy. He didn't live life exactly according to the script that was written in those days, but he was a happy man—and all because he figured out what he wanted and went after it.

The point to this story is that you too can be happy as long as you get a very clear picture of what you want. And if you can create this picture before you get into a relationship, you won't have to leave anyone behind, like Wyatt did.

Have you read *Think and Grow Rich* by Napoleon Hill? This incredibly successful classic has probably sold more copies than just about any book besides the Bible. Yet it contains some very elementary principles—information that has been given over and over in one form or another, in nearly every success program or book ever created. The main principle of Hill's book is so simple that most of us still tend to overlook it: *In order to get something, you have to have a clear-cut goal.*

Hill wrote, "Anything the mind can conceive and believe in, it can achieve." Notice the order in which the words appear in that sentence. We've begun our own journey with *conceiving* because that's where the relationship you want to create must start: not with the other person but with your conceiving in your own mind exactly what you want from a relationship. You must also conceive what you want to give *to* another person: what you bring to the table. Whatever you conceive is brought to reality by *believing* that you can create the relationship you want.

In order to believe that, you first must believe in yourself.

CONFIDENCE IS THE KEY

The program outlined in this book is designed to give you self-confidence and the courage to take risks. It is designed to help you develop the skills to achieve happiness in a relationship. You have to have confidence and skills in order to know that you're a worthy person and a worthy mate. But before we go any further with that, let's look at the other side of the coin. If confidence gives you the skills to find the right relationship, it also gives you the *strength to be able to walk away from the wrong relationship.*

So many of us have spent years in a relationship with the wrong person, someone who can never fulfill our needs, someone who can never give us contentment—and we've done this out of the fear that we won't find anyone else. The purpose of this book, then, is not only to help you find the right relationship, but to give you the confidence and assurance to walk away from the wrong one at any time.

If you have the skills and the confidence, you can find a new relationship at any time you want.

If I do nothing else in the course of this book, I am going to help you build the skills to ensure *you never become so attached to the outcome of any given relationship that you can't face the fact that the person and the relationship are wrong for you.* You have to know if and when to walk out the door—and you have to have the confidence to actually do it.

If you don't have the confidence, how can you get it? That's what we're going to explore in the first exercises in this chapter.

CREATING YOUR RELATIONSHIP JOURNAL

Since we're going to be doing exercises throughout this book, I've provided space in the appropriate places for you to jot down your responses. *If, however, you don't want to mark in the book, you should create a separate Relationship Journal.* You'll use this journal for all of the exercises, and you may also use it to make any other notes and observations along the way. A plain spiral notebook will do, or one of those decorative blank books; use whatever you're comfortable with. It's your book. What's important is that you do the exercises.

So let's get started. . . .

BELIEVING IN YOURSELF: AN EXERCISE IN SELF-WORTH

Believing in yourself can be a challenge, particularly if you've just come out of an unhappy relationship, or haven't had a date in months, or are just feeling down about yourself. The purpose of this first exercise is to help you discover what a wonderful and truly unique person you are. It's not going to magically and instantaneously transform your self-image, but it is designed to help you begin thinking of yourself in more positive terms than you may have been doing. This is a good first step toward a healthier self-image.

What you're going to do in this exercise is take an inventory of yourself. I can hear the groans out there now. How many times, especially if you're a woman, have you done an inventory of your faults? Girls are trained from the time they're little to look pretty, do better, sit up straighter, smile more. Little boys don't fare much better; they're told to be braver, be stronger, be tougher. The message we all receive is that somehow we're not good enough. Unfortunately, too many of us take this message to heart and, as we grow up, we continue to remind ourselves of our shortcomings.

It's time to put those old habits to rest. In this exercise you're going to take an inventory not of your shortcomings but of your assets. Grab a pencil and your Relationship Journal if you don't want to write in this book. Then get comfortable, turn on some appropriate background music if you wish, and begin *quickly* writing a list of all the traits you have that work for you.

Make a list of everything about you that you think is really great, or even just pretty good. Don't leave anything out. Don't just concentrate on physical appearance. Focus also on character or personality traits—decisiveness, compassion, a sense of humor—and on achievements—professional, athletic, or otherwise. Think about everything that is wonderful about you and makes you unique in all the world.

There are two keys here: be specific, and don't pause to edit. The moment the thought enters your mind write it down, without any qualifiers. But here's the challenge: don't take more than about twenty minutes on this—and by the time those twenty minutes are up, have about fifty items. That might seem like a daunting task, but it's my guess that once you really get started, you won't be able to stop.

♥ ♥ ♡ ♥ ♥ ♥ ♥ ♥ ♥ ♥ ♥ ♥ ♥

Exercise 1-1A. Inventory of Assets

My Assets

When twenty minutes are up, review your list. Now is the time to edit; narrow the list down to just ten items. These are the top ten traits that you feel are the most important to you. Take your time here, because you're going to be using this list.

♥ ♥ ♥ ♡ ♥ ♥ ♥ ♥ ♥ ♥ ♥ ♥ ♥

EXERCISE 1-1B. TOP TEN ASSETS

My Top Ten Assets

1.

2.

3.

4.

5.

6.

7.

8.

9.

10.

When you're finished, and you're satisfied with what you've done, look at your list and think about all the people in the world you know of who are in good relationships, or who are at least dating, *who don't have your first trait.* Maybe you believe your best feature is beautiful eyes. Now think about the dozens of people you know or know of who are dating, but who have perfectly unremarkable eyes. Or perhaps your number one trait is that you're a witty and eloquent woman. Think about that little airhead you know at the gym, whose conversational skills seem limited to giggles and one-syllable words. She's not too bright, but she's dating, isn't she? Obviously you have a trait that she lacks. Or maybe you know someone who seems to be self-centered or humorless or insensitive—which you're not, of course—but *that* person is dating.

Please know that your objective here is not to pick on the negative traits of others, but to focus on the fact that *you* have a lot to offer, and there's no one in the world exactly like you.

Now here's how you can put this "top ten" list of your best traits to use immediately. First, take it on the road with you. Place the list in your wallet or purse so it will be within easy reach whenever you step out of the house. When you enter an office or restaurant or party and see someone who you think is more extroverted than you, more gregarious, better looking—whichever trait, real or imagined—the physical presence of your list will help you remember you have a lot going for you, too.

This is the first step to gaining confidence, a sound basis on which to attract another person. *You have to attract someone by believing in yourself.* You have to have something that shines from within, from your very center. Sometimes you just need a reminder, and that's the purpose of keeping this list with you.

I suggest you also use the list to create an affirmation based on your top traits. Begin every day by saying your affirmation to yourself, e.g., *I'm pretty. I'm smart. I'm caring.* Whatever is on the list, incorporate it into your affirmation. My friend Joan, for example, uses these words: "I love who I am, I'm grounded in my power and I'm secure on all levels."

Maybe you think affirmations are sort of silly. After all, they're just words, aren't they? How can repeating a few words to yourself every day possibly make any difference in your life?

It's true that affirmations are "just" words, but words can set great events in motion. Words can inspire people to take action, and this applies to the words you say to yourself just as truly as it applies to the speech of any great orator. The key is to write an affirmation that really says what you want it to say, and then truly listen to yourself every time you repeat it. Take time to ponder on the meaning of the words. Act "as if" you believe them, and soon you will. If you don't do this, then yes, an affirmation can become just a meaningless series of words. But use your affirmation the way it was intended, and I can promise you that it will be very powerful.

Once you've created your affirmation, repeat it to yourself first thing in the morning while looking in the mirror, when you're putting on your makeup or shaving. The goal is to get yourself into a mental state of self-confidence, before you even walk out your front door.

Okay, are you ready? It's time to create your own personal affirmation.

♥ ♥ ♥ ♥ ♡ ♥ ♥ ♥ ♥ ♥ ♥ ♥ ♥

EXERCISE 1-1C. PERSONAL AFFIRMATION

My Affirmation

THE SECRET THAT CAN GIVE YOU THE EDGE

Now that you have created and are using your top ten list and your affirmation, you're on the road to a healthy self-image. But old habits die hard, and occasionally you still may find that you're comparing yourself to other people. Here's a "secret tip" that may help you overcome this habit once and for all. If you wish, write this down and put it in your wallet along with your top ten list:

The top factor making people successful and allowing them to achieve is not their capability . . . but their state of mind.

How many people have you seen who are successful, but seem to have far less to work with than you do? What makes them successful? If you study them closely, I bet you'll find that the key to their success is that they have a great attitude. Their state of mind makes all the difference.

That's why you absolutely must get yourself into an optimal state of mind. You must develop a willingness to believe in yourself. This is what is truly important before you can even begin to imagine the life you want, to say nothing of actually going out and getting it.

You've created your top ten list and your affirmation; now get out there and use them.

BUT WHAT DO I DO ABOUT THOSE TRAITS THAT AREN'T SO GREAT?

We all have areas we want to improve in our lives—a weight problem, perhaps, or shyness, or a long-standing pattern of self-defeating behavior. Even people who seem to "have it all" have characteristics that nag at them, or pull them down, or that they simply think they should improve.

For a colleague of mine, named Tina, that nagging problem is ten pounds. Tina is gorgeous and bright and successful, yet she struggles with those few pounds constantly. When her weight is "perfect" (by her definition) she feels there's nothing in the world she can't achieve. On the other hand, when she has those extra pounds, she has a tendency to blame them if anything goes wrong in her life. You may think that ten pounds is a trivial matter, but it's not trivial to Tina. Let's say she is going to do a radio show and knows she has those few extra pounds. It doesn't matter that no one can even see her on the radio (and even if they could they wouldn't perceive those ten pounds—she's tall and has a terrific figure), but that she knows the extra weight is there and that it nags at her. So Tina *does* something about the problem. Rather than stewing over it, she sets a specific goal for herself to lose those ten pounds. She watches her diet a bit more carefully and steps up her exercise routine. And before she knows it she's back at her ideal weight.

I'm sure you can think of a few areas in which you'd like to improve yourself. Perhaps you're not up on current events, so when you're at a party and people start to talk about what's going on with some controversial legislation, you feel at a loss. Or maybe, like Tina, you're struggling with a few extra pounds. Whatever is nagging at you, whatever is eroding your self-image—that's what we're going to concentrate on in this next exercise. The way to deal with these nagging problems is not to sweep them under the rug, or to condemn yourself, but to face them honestly and do something about them.

In your Relationship Journal or in the space provided in this book, make a list of all your personal traits that you consider liabilities. Then, right beside each item, write some step you can take to improve. No matter what it is, no matter how superficial it seems, if it bothers you, put it on the list and make a plan to do something small to improve it.

It's important not to make grandiose, unrealistic plans. You'll only set yourself up for failure and end up more frustrated than you were before. The secret is to start small, but do take action: set yourself up for success.

Life is a constant process of change. You are always getting better or you're getting worse, but you will not stay the same. It's your choice.

Okay, it's time to make your list.

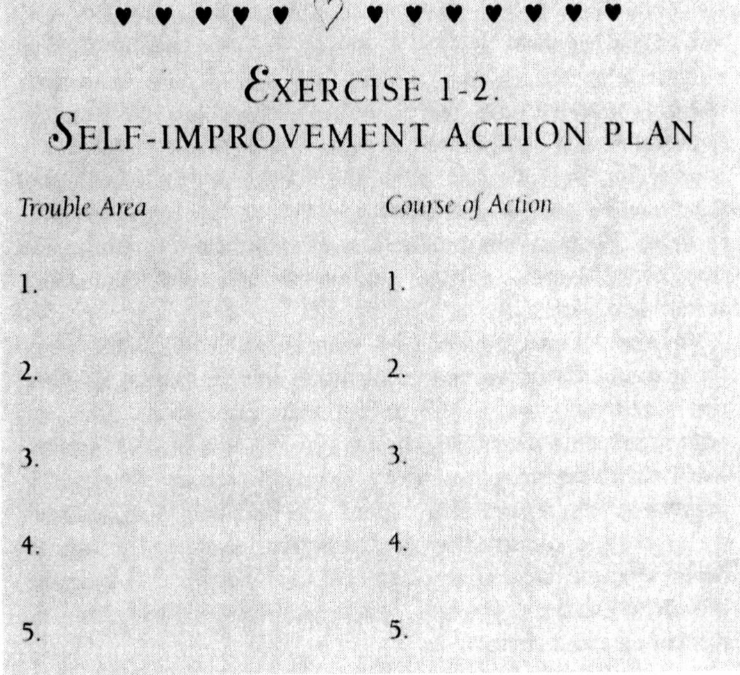

Exercise 1-2. Self-Improvement Action Plan

Trouble Area	*Course of Action*
1.	1.
2.	2.
3.	3.
4.	4.
5.	5.

PAIN OR PLEASURE? A TOOL FOR STAYING "ON THE PATH"

Making a list of your liabilities and the actions you can take to improve them is a very good beginning, but actually carrying out your intentions is another matter. It may help you to understand how motivation works, and then to apply that understanding by using a powerful tool: your imagination.

Anthony Robbins has said that people are controlled by the twin forces of pain and pleasure—but most people will do more to avoid pain than they ever will to gain pleasure. The threat of loss is, for most people, a much stronger motivation than the promise of a reward.

If you're not convinced, consider this example. What do you imagine would spur you to take the most immediate and drastic action to improve your financial situation: the thought that, if you were earning more money, you might be able to buy or build your dream home, or the fear of getting thrown out of your present apartment because you couldn't pay the rent? You might or might not be inspired to start moonlighting in order to save for the down payment on your dream castle—but, if you're like most people, you'd go to some lengths to keep from getting thrown out on the streets; you'd take on a second or even a third job if you had to. *People will do just about anything to avoid losing what they already have.*

You may be saying, "This is all very interesting, but how does it apply to my quest for self-improvement, and, for that matter, to my search for a relationship?" Well, you bought this book because, presumably, you want to find a healthy, lasting relationship. You want to make your life better. *If these changes don't happen, you are going to have a loss.* If you truly understand this, you can use your fear of loss as a tool to help motivate you to action.

"But how can I get worked up over 'losing' something that I don't have in the first place?" you're probably asking. That's a good question. The thought of loss is not a very powerful motivator if you're not able to truly conceive how *much* of a loss you're facing. And if you've never experienced even moderate success in improving your life, you may feel that, in fact, you have little to lose. If this is the case, how can the prospect of loss possibly move you to action?

This is where visualization, or imagination, comes into play.

Imagine, for example, that you've accomplished the number one self-improvement goal on the list you just made. Let's say you're a woman who's just lost those ten pounds that had been nagging at you. Picture yourself walking into a party wearing a slinky red dress; imagine a roomful of admiring male (and envious female) eyes on you. Keep on imagining, and envision yourself meeting, at that very party, the man who turns out to be your soul mate. . . .

Or perhaps your goal was to become more outgoing so that you wouldn't feel so awkward and out of place at parties, and toward that end you've been working to sharpen your conversational skills. Imagine yourself, then, engaged in lively discourse at a cocktail party. Whereas you were formerly quiet and shy, now you find yourself delighting, and being delighted by, everyone you talk to at that party. Now take it a step further and imagine this is an office party, where your boss notices for the first time what a dynamic and intelligent person you are. Next thing you know, you're being offered a promotion and a handsome raise. . . .

These are fairly extreme examples, but their purpose is to get you to start thinking. Substitute your own goals, of course. The trick is to use your imagination to create a detailed, believable scenario, and to *feel the feelings*. Really try to experience the pride and sense of accomplishment that comes with reaching your goal. Imagine all the rewards—social, emotional, financial—that could be yours were you to make the change or changes you envision. *Imagine having it all.*

Then imagine losing it all, or never having it in the first place—never losing the weight, never doing anything to improve your conversational skills, and, as a result, not feeling confident enough to go to that party (or wherever). Take the wonderful scenario you imagined previously and imagine the opposite—and *try to really feel the loss.* The fact is, in this scenario, you're no worse off than you are right now or than you were before trying to reach your goals.

I would suggest you use the above exercise in imagination as often as you need to, in order to truly convince yourself you're losing out by not taking action to improve the areas that are bothering you. Most important to the focus of this book, *you may be missing out on that great relationship you want in your life.* I'll be the first to acknowledge that taking new steps can be scary but, to me, the prospect of losing out on happiness is much more frightening than the thought of, say, simply going to a party and not having a good time one night.

IT'S ALL ABOUT FOCUS

Few of the improvements you want to make are going to happen overnight and, during the course of your self-improvement campaign, you may have some setbacks. You can take steps to keep these to a minimum by learning how to focus.

A man I know, whom I'll call Rick, was recently hired by a large ad agency. His new position requires that he give frequent presentations to clients. In the past this would have been a real challenge because, although Rick is brilliant, talented, and creative, for many years he had a severe stuttering problem, which made him very self-conscious. Ongoing speech therapy and his own determined efforts have helped him nearly overcome the problem, but he is still very aware of his limitations. "Whenever I get in front of a room to make a presentation I have a choice," Rick told me. "I can do one of two things: I can dwell on what I feel is a flaw in my speech, or I can focus my attention on the content of my presentation and how my ideas can benefit the client. I've learned to make myself do the latter. I'm still aware of my past speech problems, but I'm also very proud of my progress. I've learned to compensate by talking a bit more slowly than most people do, and pausing often. And when I pause, I do it in a way that appears to be for effect. My presentations are always a success because I'm really concentrating on what I'm doing right, not on my personal flaws. This increases my confidence, and clients notice that and respond to it."

Rick's focus has made all the difference. He's learned that focus is the key to one's state of mind and, as such, it is the key to self-confidence.

Rick has also learned something else about confidence: it is an inside job. Rick feels that, more than anything else—even the speech therapy—his own determination and belief in himself have been the factors enabling him to overcome his liability.

"Confidence is enforced by the responses of others, of course, but it begins inside," he states. "And it all begins with where you put your focus." Just as Rick has done, you must learn to put your focus on the good.

Here's another secret: *your thoughts are a powerful force in your life.* Most of the events in our lives do not "just" happen; virtually everything begins with thoughts. Thoughts produce feelings, and feelings, in turn, produce actions. But what produces the thoughts in the first place?

That's right: your focus.

LIVING IN THE NOW

As we mentioned previously, you may face setbacks in your quest for self-improvement. But setbacks don't have to mean failure. When you're facing a setback, don't think about what you haven't done yet; think about what you *have* accomplished. Don't stop your life because you haven't reached your goal. Concentrate on what you have going for you now.

Have you heard the old saying that "getting there is half the fun"? There's a lot of truth in that; when it comes right down to it, everything is about the journey. Each day is the only day you have, so your passion for life has to be there *on that day*. You want to summon up all the passion you possibly can to get you on the road to being better, being happier, and living a more healthy and vital life.

Now it's time to broaden your scope a little bit. You have a better sense of yourself; it's time to start focusing on what you want in a relationship. That's the purpose of the next exercises.

FINDING OUT WHAT YOU WANT: AN EXERCISE IN GOAL-SETTING

In a way, we're right back where we started: everything begins with knowing what you want. Now that you know a little bit more about who you are, you're much better qualified to determine what you want. You are working from a position of strength and self-esteem. You are not going to "settle"; you're going to go for what you truly want and deserve.

Take a few moments and think about your life in the last five years. In the last five years, have there been things that you really wanted to do but didn't, some plans you'd made that didn't work out, some dream you had that never became reality?

Let's say you wanted to go back to school and get your degree, but it didn't happen. Well, what did happen? What kept you from achieving your dream? More than likely it was that old bugaboo, procrastination. Or perhaps you simply got caught up in the events of your life: a child got ill, you got overloaded at work, or you had family problems. Something happened—you got sidetracked and continued to put it off.

You might be able to offer all sorts of reasons, but look at it honestly: could the essential problem be that the commitment just wasn't there?

Commitment is your pledge to take action. Most likely you didn't get your degree because your plan, and therefore your pledge, weren't there. Perhaps you just weren't convinced that you really needed or wanted the degree, even though it probably would have resulted in a better-paying job. It was easier to settle into a lower paying (albeit safe and routine) job. You may have sometimes felt dissatisfied with your choice, but you always appeased yourself with the thought, in the back of your mind, that you'd eventually go back to school.

You may have found, however, that as time goes by it has become more difficult to pull yourself out of your routine, while it's become easier to find excuses not to get your degree.

If you had had a plan, if you'd conceived what you wanted from the beginning, you may very well have reached your goal by now.

Having a plan is important, but I want to go a step further and add that it's also *vitally important to put your plan in writing.* As everyone from Napoleon Hill to Stephen Covey would agree, you can only achieve something if you have first conceived it in your mind—and writing it down makes it more "real."

Before you begin writing, however, you must determine where

you are right now, and where you want to go from here. Maybe you've just broken up from a relationship and you're devastated. You simply want to get over that person and start to meet new people. Perhaps you just want to get out of the house. Or maybe you want to attract a partner who is going to be your lifelong soul mate.

Whatever your goal is, write it down. But please do not write it down without first considering it carefully. For example, don't write that you want to attract your lifelong mate if you haven't even had a date in a year or so. The point of this exercise is to *really get in touch with where you are now.*

You're going to write two different goals: your short-term goal, which covers the next ninety days; and your long-term goal, covering anywhere from the next six months to the next two years. It depends upon the length of time your mind can realistically conceptualize. If you can't imagine your life twenty-four months from now, if the longest interval you can imagine is six months, work with the interval you're comfortable with. You're not writing a fairy tale; *goals are really supposed to be predictions of your future.* You want to think big, certainly, but you also want to think realistically.

Not only is it important that you write clearly, concisely, and realistically, but *it's important for you to write a date.* This is another way of making the goal more "real," but it's more than that. Our minds seem to work better if there's a time limit. Let's say you're thinking of writing a book—but you never specify when you want to begin or complete it. Your mind never gets the message to the unconscious. More than likely, you're never even going to begin that book.

It's the same with creating a relationship or anything else you want in your life. You need to write down a date to spur your mind to get the message to the unconscious. You can change the date later if you wish; you're not engraving anything in stone. Just make sure you do write down that date.

To prepare for this exercise it might help you to set the stage, mentally. After all, you're creating magic here, and you want to set up the best conditions for doing so. Take a break from your reading again and get into a state where you can clearly visualize what will really make you happy. Sit back in a comfortable place, put on some soft pleasant music if you wish, and close your eyes.

I've found that visualization really does help make this exercise much more effective. Visualize yourself being happy. It may help to remember a time (or times) when you were truly joyful. Perhaps it was long ago, when you were a child and your father was able to make it home from a long business trip in order to be with the family on Thanksgiving. Or maybe it was when the guy you had such a crush on in high school asked you to the prom. Or perhaps your joy was of a more material nature—e.g., buying your first car—or maybe it was truly profound, such as a religious or mystical experience. It doesn't matter; the point is to get yourself into that blissful state where you feel completely content and happy. Imagine a condition in which all your needs are met and you feel real joy.

Then open your eyes and start writing. As usual, I've provided space in the book, but if you don't want to mark on the pages just turn to some clean pages in your Relationship Journal and set them up the way I've set up the exercise pages.

Once you've done this, write a brief plan to get what you want. For example, let's suppose you're a guy whose short-term goal is to date two attractive women within thirty days. What steps can you take to make this more likely to happen? You can start small. Let's say you're an avid reader. Perhaps you can plan on going to the next Singles Night at your local bookstore/café. These events are quite popular, and you're almost guaranteed to meet at least a few women who share your interests. Or suppose your long-term goal is to get married and start a family within the next two years. What can you do that will bring you closer to that goal? If you're comfortable with it, you might consider joining a dating service, specifying that your goal is marriage and a family. Or actively engage your friends in your search; have them introduce you to people. Just come up with a realistic plan of action that will truly help you reach your goal.

Well, are you ready? Sit back, get comfortable, put on some music and get into a state of visualizing your joy. And then get started writing.

♥ ♥ ♥ ♥ ♥ ♥ ♡ ♥ ♥ ♥ ♥ ♥ ♥

EXERCISE 1-3. SHORT-TERM RELATIONSHIP GOALS

Write down what you want to achieve within the next thirty days (e.g., I, Barbara Smith, want to date two to three attractive men in the next thirty days).

I, ______________________________

want ______________________________

____

by (date)______________________________

My plan to get what I want:

____

____

____

____

♥ ♥ ♥ ♥ ♥ ♥ ♥ ♡ ♥ ♥ ♥ ♥ ♥

EXERCISE 1-4. LONG-TERM RELATIONSHIP GOALS

Write down what you want to achieve within the next one to three years (e.g., I, Bill Johnson, want to be married and start a family by the end of 1998).

I, ______________________________

want, ______________________________

____

by (date)______________________________

My plan to get what I want:

____

____

____

____

WHAT KIND OF PERSON DO YOU WANT TO ATTRACT? MAKING YOUR "PARTNER WISH LIST"

You've explored who you are and have begun seriously considering what, in general, you want in a relationship; now it's time to focus on the person you want to attract. As a matter of fact, this is the place where most people start out, and that's why they're so often unsuccessful. They haven't laid the groundwork for attracting that perfect person.

Well, you've done your groundwork and you're ready to move on. What's the next step? It's time to start thinking about specific qualities in the person you're looking for. It's impossible to attract the right person for you if you have no idea what the right person is like. If that sounds familiar, it's because it's a variation on our theme for this section: You can't get what you want until you *know* what you want.

That's why I've devised a simple way to help you start attracting the person you want. You're going to do this by writing down exactly what that person is going to be like. You will create a series of simple "wish lists" to help you decide what kind of person you want to attract. Then you're going to do a wish list to imagine the kind of couple you want the two of you to be.

To help inspire you, I'll be sharing with you several "relationship wish lists" from various men and women I've worked with (all the names have been changed, of course). Keep your lists as simple as they've kept theirs. Be spontaneous and only include the things that are very important to you. If you wish to add more items or details later you can, but keep your initial lists simple. And don't discount the importance of this exercise just because you're "making it up," that is, listing the attributes of a person you haven't even met yet. Remember, "writing it down" can be a very powerful tool in helping to turn your dreams into reality. Besides, this exercise is *fun*.

The first part of your wish list will specify the type of person you want in your life. Again, you may use the pages provided in this book, or pages in your Relationship Journal. Divide this part into four sections, with one page for each section:

1. The man or woman I want is (general characteristics and traits such as age, height, profession, parental status, etc.)
2. His/her interests are (reading, exercising, outdoor sports, etc.)
3. How he/she feels about me, and how he/she expresses it (he respects me, she cherishes me, he compliments me about something every day, she listens to me, etc.)
4. His/her general attitude is (he is optimistic about life, she is adventurous, he is ambitious but balanced, she loves animals, etc.)

Suzanne is a real estate broker in her early forties. Here's her list for the first item on the partner wish list, "general characteristics."

The man I want is:

1. Forty-five years or older.
2. Six feet or taller.
3. A person who exercises.
4. A person who has been married.
5. Someone who doesn't want any more children, though it's okay if he already has children.
6. Confident.
7. A person who does well in his work and likes what he does.
8. A person who has a good sense of humor.
9. A person who does not smoke.
10. A person who doesn't over-drink and is not addicted to drugs.

That's a pretty reasonable list, isn't it? Even so, Suzanne has told me, there may be one or two items on which she's willing to negotiate. "Here's the way I look at it," she says. "I'm working to attract the person who is perfect for me, and I'm changing and becoming better so I can do that—but the universe, or my higher power, or my God, or whatever you want to call it, knows more than I do and may end up sending me somebody who doesn't match my list perfectly." That's a reflection of Suzanne's beliefs, of course, and if you don't share a belief in God or a higher power, that's okay. But she has a good point, which is that things don't always turn out exactly the way we expect. So perhaps when you do attract that "perfect" person, there may be a few items you'll have to negotiate on.

For example, let's take item number 2 on Suzanne's list. Imagine she's met this terrific guy who has all the other qualities she listed, except he's only five-feet-nine. Is that something she can live with? "Absolutely!" she says with emphasis. "I'm five-nine myself, but there's no law that says the man of my dreams HAS to be taller than I am." Or take the fourth item: suppose this man has never been married, but he's had a long-term live-in relationship that accomplished the same thing in determining his capacity for intimacy. That would mean just as much as if there had been a ceremony to formalize his relationship, so Suzanne feels she could probably negotiate on that item. "When I was making my list," she explains, "the phrases 'six feet or taller' and 'has been married' were simply thoughts that came up spontaneously, so I wrote them down." Be similarly spontaneous with your list.

Certain items on Suzanne's list are not negotiable. The smoking issue may not be a negotiable one for her. Suzanne is health-conscious, and besides that, she is allergic to cigarette smoke. "Even if he didn't smoke in my presence," she says, "I would want a life partner who cared enough about his health not to smoke at all; after all, I want him to be around for a long time."

So go ahead and make your list, and, since you're being spontaneous, don't worry at this point about whether a given item is negotiable or not.

♥ ♥ ♥ ♥ ♥ ♥ ♥ ♥ ♡ ♥ ♥ ♥ ♥

Exercise 1-5A. Partner Wish List

The man/woman I want is/has

(e.g., is forty-five years or older, is physically fit, has children, likes animals, has a dry sense of humor.)

The next step is to imagine what your partner's interests are. What does he like to do? How does she like to spend her time? David, a thirty-eight-year-old architect, wrote this for item 2 on the wish list:

The woman I want is interested in:

1. Everything!—in short, she has great curiosity.
2. Reading.
3. Plays, movies, and music (recorded and live).
4. Exercise (but she's not obsessive about it).
5. Travel.
6. Dancing (occasionally).
7. Parties; prefers small parties to large, but is comfortable at either.

You'll notice David's first item is, "has great curiosity." For David, it would be very difficult to negotiate on that. "I have found," he says (and I agree with his observation), "that people are either generally curious or not, and the point of determination seems to be about the age of thirty. If someone is still curious at thirty, they're going to be that way at ninety." David is stimulated by people who are constantly seeking to expand their horizons.

"I'm aware," he continues, "that many folks are more comfortable in a small radius. But I really tend to hang around people who live their lives on a broader scale." Recently David met a woman who has many of the traits on his first list. Besides being very attractive, she's the right age and height, and has all of the character traits he wants in a life partner. But she lives in a small town in east Texas, goes to church on Sunday, bowls on Wednesday, goes to a movie on Friday night. And she's perfectly happy with her life; her goal is to get married, settle down in her hometown, and raise a family. She has no desire to travel at all.

"There's absolutely nothing wrong with that," says David. "It's a very secure, safe, and predictable lifestyle. For me, though, it would be a very boring lifestyle. I want to settle down and get married, too, but I also want to travel the world with my wife."

Does this mean that his friend's small-town lifestyle is "wrong"?

No, of course not. On the other hand, is it "wrong" for David to be a curious person, and to want to surround himself with others who are curious? No. There's no value judgment either way; all it means is that David and his small-town friend aren't harmonious lifelong mates.

Well, enough about David. Pick up your pencil, and start your second list.

♥ ♥ ♥ ♥ ♥ ♥ ♥ ♥ ♥ ♥ ♡ ♥ ♥

Exercise 1-5B. Partner Wish List

His/her interests are

(e.g., reading, exercising, traveling, buying antiques.)

Now it's time to think about how your ideal partner feels about you. Even though we're still working in the realm of imagination, this step is particularly important. It's one ingredient that many people leave out when they're considering what they want in a mate. Don't make that mistake. You want somebody who loves you as much as you love them, and who expresses that love in a way that meets your needs. Linda, a thirty-two-year-old artist, writes:

How the man I want feels about me, and expresses those feelings:

1. He's crazy about me; he adores me.
2. He thinks I'm beautiful, funny, and intelligent.
3. He trusts me.
4. He is affectionate with me.
5. He's proud of me.
6. We have a wonderful sex life.
7. He has things to teach me.
8. He has a few good friends that he's had long-term relationships with (this shows me that he cares about, and is capable of sustaining, long-term relationships).
9. He is supportive, tender, and caring toward me.

"This is such an important area," says Linda, "that I'm not really willing to negotiate on any of these items."

Linda has a good point. How your partner feels about you is every bit as important as his or her vital statistics or interests—if not more so. What you write in this section is a direct reflection of your self-esteem. Very simply, you want a partner who loves you as much as you love yourself.

So pick up your pencil and start filling in your own list.

♥ ♥ ♥ ♥ ♥ ♥ ♥ ♥ ♥ ♡ ♥ ♥ ♥

Exercise 1-5C. Partner Wish List

How he/she feels about me, and expresses those feelings

(e.g., she respects me; he adores me; she listens to me without criticism; he gives me compliments.)

You've determined your ideal partner's qualities, interests, and attitudes toward you. The last piece in this part of the puzzle is this: what you want your partner's attitudes toward life to be. Ted, a thirty-six-year-old humanities professor at a small university, came up with this list:

The attitudes of the woman I want:

1. She is interested in, and accepting of, people from other cultures.
2. She believes in God, but is tolerant of all religions.
3. She is a loyal friend.
4. She is honest and ethical.
5. She is generous.
6. She drinks moderately, if at all.
7. She has a healthy interest in politics and world affairs.
8. She is a feminist but she likes, respects, and trusts men.

As was the case with Linda and the previous list, Ted is not really willing to negotiate on the items on this list. "To me," he explains, "these traits reflect a potential partner's personality and, in some cases, her character. I try not to place a negative value judgment on a woman who doesn't meet the above criteria, beyond deciding that she is probably not the life partner for me." When I asked Ted to give me an example he said, "Well, I very much believe in God and consider myself a Christian. But I've made an extensive study of world religions and I find truth in all of them. I *don't* believe in a God who is going to send to hell all the people who don't believe in one specific religion. It just doesn't compute for me. So I probably wouldn't be very compatible as a life partner to somebody who was not tolerant of people of other faiths."

As Ted has realized, this is another area you need to consider carefully. So get started on your own list.

♥ ♥ ♥ ♥ ♥ ♥ ♥ ♥ ♡ ♥ ♥ ♥ ♥

Exercise 1-5D. Partner Wish List

His/her attitudes toward life

(e.g., he is an incurable optimist; she is ambitious but balanced; he is adventurous.)

By now you may have a much clearer idea of the kind of person you want to attract in your life. You are going to perfect this more as time goes along, but this was your way of sending that first message to yourself, throwing the first pebble out into the lake, and, if you're comfortable with this concept, making the first ripple in the universe.

It is a real first step in attracting that person to you.

WHAT KIND OF COUPLE ARE YOU GOING TO BE?

Now it's time to go a step further. Consider this "perfect person" you've been dreaming up in the last few pages, and start thinking about how the two of you are going to be together, as a couple. Use the space in this book, or pages in your Relationship Journal. Head the page very simply, with the word "we," for that's what this next section is all about. You're no longer just thinking of "me" or "him" or "her"—you're thinking about "we." Rachel, a twenty-eight-year-old image consultant, writes:

We . . .

1. Resolve conflict well with each other.
2. Have fun and are playful.
3. Have passion and tenderness in our lovemaking.
4. Have stimulating philosophical and political conversations.
5. Are supportive and nurturing of each other in a loving and reciprocal way.
6. Give each other room to grow and change within our relationship.

That's how Rachel sees herself as part of a couple. You may see yourself quite differently. But really think about this, and make it as real as you can.

♥ ♥ ♥ ♥ ♥ ♥ ♥ ♡ ♥ ♥ ♥ ♥ ♥

Exercise 1-6. Couple Wish List

We . . .

(e.g., we are an inspiration to other couples; we are kind and loving toward one another's families; we laugh a lot; we resolve conflicts quickly.)

SEALED WITH A WISH . . . AND ANOTHER AFFIRMATION

Now I have a couple of final exercises for you. These are optional, but I really suggest you do them. Don't write them in this book or in your Relationship Journal; keep them to yourself.

The first exercise will take you back to your childhood, when you made secret wishes that you never told anybody. This is a similar exercise in imagination, and I think it's a lot of fun.

The rule is, your wish has to be about something very specific—an ideal scenario you'd like to happen. Veronica, a thirty-one-year-old editorial assistant at a national magazine, shared with me her "secret" wish: *"After we've been dating a year, my perfect person will want to marry me; we'll find a beautiful home together and take a glorious honeymoon to Venice, France, or Switzerland."* I say, more power to Veronica. Make up your own exciting, romantic scenario, but remember to keep it to yourself. Take a few moments to do this. . . .

♥ ♥ ♥

. . . and now that you have made your "secret wish," your last exercise before we sign off in this chapter is to write a simple affirmation statement. This is a little different from the affirmation you wrote earlier. This one will be a validation of all the work you've been doing in this section. It is an affirmation that you have set some marvelous events in motion in your life. Let me give you an example:

I, [name], am now attracting the kind of person and relationship that is ideal for me, the perfect one for me.

Your affirmation can be similar in structure and content, but the point is to make it meaningful and satisfying for you. So tailor it to your own needs and feel comfortable saying it.

USING THE PRINCIPLES IN THIS CHAPTER

You've done a lot of work in this chapter; I suggest you rest awhile before you go on to the next chapter on *Contentment*. But it's never too soon to begin practicing what we've discussed so far. Here's how you can make this practice part of your everyday life:

- *Study and take to heart that list you made of the "top ten" terrific things about you*. Look at your inventory of assets when you wake up in the morning, so that you start the day feeling confident and good about yourself, knowing what you have to offer in a relationship.
- *Use that affirmation you created from your inventory of assets*. Study your goals and follow up on your plans of action.
- *Keep in mind those "wish lists" you made for your partner and relationship*. Go back over your lists and fine-tune them if you wish. Spend as much time "cleaning them up" as you need to before you go on to the next chapter.

We've only covered the first principle, the first step. There's a distance to go yet. But you're off to a good start—and from now on you're on a ride you can't stop, unless you quit participating.

It's really all about choice. By beginning and continuing on this journey, you are making the choice to participate in life. You are choosing to take action, to get over your fears, and to find the right person for you, the perfect relationship for you.

You should be proud of yourself for making that choice.

♥ The Second Principle ♥

Contentment

Contentment in a relationship means getting your needs satisfied. Men and women have different needs, and unless all of those needs are met, the relationship is not going to be truly satisfying to either partner.

If you've done all of the exercises in chapter one, you probably have a good general idea of who you are and what you *want* in a relationship. It's time now to get more specific about *needs.*

Don't worry if you have yet to even *meet* your partner; in fact, so much the better: it's really best to have this information going into a relationship.

Now, before we go any further, I wish to clarify what I mean by "needs" and "relationship." In this chapter, and throughout this book, we are focusing on your relationship with your significant other. Whether you're married or not, this relationship is unlike any other in your life.

Unfortunately, many intimate relationships fail because people expect to have *all* of their needs met by their partner. That's a pretty large burden to place on a person or on a relationship. The truth is that *no one person can meet all of your needs.*

Suppose, for example, that you're an avid tennis player, but the person you fall madly in love with and marry has little interest in the game. You also have a close friend with whom you've played tennis for years. It wouldn't be reasonable to expect your loved one to fulfill your need for a tennis partner—and there's absolutely no reason for you to discontinue your weekly tennis game with your friend. There's nothing wrong with going outside of your intimate relationship to meet this kind of need.

There are certain needs, however, that only the significant other in your life can really fulfill, and if that person fails to meet these needs—ANY OF THEM AT ALL—you will not feel content. You may always feel that something is missing in the relationship. These are the needs we're going to be talking about in this chapter.

Let's explore these needs in detail.

HER NEEDS

The woman sets the level and tone of how happy the relationship is going to be. That's why I'm covering women's needs first.

You've probably seen those T-shirts and coffee mugs that say, "If Mama ain't happy, nobody's happy." There's a lot of truth to that little saying. On the other hand, if a woman's needs are met, inevitably she meets many of her partner's needs.

This does not mean that a woman doesn't have to work at making her partner happy, or that she instinctively knows what to do, whereas the poor guy has to figure everything out. It is simply that *much of a man's happiness in a relationship hinges on his feeling that he is making the woman he loves happy.*

In other words, *a man is generally happy if his woman is happy*. Rightly or wrongly, he takes responsibility for her happiness, and if she's happy, he feels successful. If he's had a great day at work and comes home to find her with a frown on her face, guess what happens? His mood plummets. He's probably not going to feel good for the rest of the evening, or even the next day when he goes to work, *because he's not going to think he's winning*. He's not going to feel successful.

A song from the musical *Camelot* asks the plaintive question: "What *do* these creatures want?" It's my guess that men have been asking this question about women since the beginning of language. If you're a man, pay close attention to this list, because I think it's going to help solve the mystery for you. Herewith, a woman's top seven needs in a relationship:

1. *To feel secure*

This is a woman's first and foremost need, dating at least from cave-dweller times. It's probably in our hard-wiring. This makes sense; for most of human history, men provided the physical or financial security. In ways that were directly tied to physical survival, they made their females feel secure.

It's not so simple these days. Many women make a living for themselves. The basics of survival and safety—in our industrialized society, at any rate—no longer depend upon the brute strength of the hunter or warrior. Some inner-city dwellers may argue that point, but overall, "security" has taken on a different, more abstract meaning. Women don't look to men as much for physical or financial security anymore; *they look to them for emotional security*.

This can be difficult for men, because traditionally all a man had to do was provide the shelter, show up for the meals, pay the bills—and he was a winner. Now that the sex roles have become more blurred, and now that it's possible for a woman to make more money than a man, where does that leave the man? If it is still his job in the relationship to make her feel secure, how can he do it? What, in fact, do we mean by "emotional security"?

Security means that a woman feels safe and protected—from danger, from harm, and from anxiety. Isn't that a contradiction of what we just said above? No. *What emotional security really means to a woman is that she can count on her man*. She needs to feel secure in his love, secure in the knowledge that he genuinely cares for her. She must feel he's *her* man, and that both of them are secure enough in the relationship to take it to the stage where commitment occurs.

For a woman, emotional security within a relationship has several aspects:

- *Her attractiveness to him:* A woman needs to feel that her man finds her the most attractive woman in his world. *This is a tremendous need for virtually ALL women.* She must feel beautiful—and it really only counts if the man in her life makes her feel that way. Everyone else in the world can tell her that she is beautiful, but if *he* doesn't feel that way, and let her know he feels that way, she's not truly secure.
- *His fidelity to her:* A woman needs to feel secure that her man is not going to stray. Even though he might look admiringly at another woman, she knows he would never act on it.
- *Emotional support:* She has to feel secure in the knowledge that when she has a "down" day emotionally, he will be there to really listen to her. He not only recognizes that it's a down day, but he also realizes that, because she's a woman, she is perhaps

> more directly in touch with her emotions, or at least more prone to express them. She may even tend to exaggerate, perhaps saying, "No one cares about me!"—when all she means is that her friend didn't return a phone call in time, and all she really wants is to be reassured that she is important.

For true emotional support to occur, a bit of mutual empathy is certainly in order in these situations. A woman may need to realize that, to her man, she will sometimes seem overly emotional. And the man needs to look at the situation—and his woman's reaction to it—and gauge in more objective terms what's going on; *at the same time, he must never make her think her feelings are invalid.*

This may seem like a pretty fine line to walk, but all a man really needs to do is to be supportive and reassuring. He can hold and comfort her by saying, "It will be fine. Everything will be okay." A man who knows his woman will know what she needs to make her feel secure and safe. It's really not so complicated after all.

I should stress, however, that most of our security and self-esteem comes from inside ourselves. A man, no matter how loving and supportive he is, simply cannot create something that is not already there. Nevertheless, as females, we still look to the man in our life to make us feel secure, to make us feel safe and protected.

Men have a big job, but it's not an impossible one. And if a man really knows his woman, it's not even that difficult. Almost certainly it will be the most rewarding job he's ever undertaken.

2. *To feel that she's number one in your life.*

This is related to the first need. Being a number one priority to each other is what the marriage ceremony is all about. Marriage is a formal expression of commitment; *it means that the two people put each other first.* They put each other before their work, before their children, before their families. They are each other's number one consideration.

Married or not, in order for a woman to feel content in a relationship, she must feel she's more important than the man's work, more important than his friends, more important than fishing or golf.

This doesn't mean that you have no outside interests. To the contrary, if you're in a relationship with a supportive woman who's also trying to meet *your* needs, she's going to bend over backward to see that you are happy. She'll understand that you need companionship with other males, that you may want to go fishing or play golf on occasion, that you want to spend time with your family, that you may occasionally have to work weekends. She'll support you in getting all of your needs met.

But she will only be truly supportive if she feels that she is the number one priority in your life. As long as she feels that you place her first, she will seldom put you to a test.

How do you show her she's number one? There are all kinds of little ways; for example, perhaps you make arrangements to take her to a doctor's appointment that's had her quite concerned—at a time when you'd normally be at work. Even if it's not such a big deal to you to change your schedule, it will make her feel so loved and so special that she'll go out of her way to make you happy you've done it.

3. *Attention*

Again, this is related to the first two items, but it's a bit more situation-specific than making a woman feel emotionally secure or making her feel she's the central priority in your life. *From time to time a woman needs her man's total attention focused on her.* I'm amazed whenever a man claims he doesn't know how to give a woman the attention she needs—yet during the pursuit stage, when he hasn't gone to bed with the woman yet, when he feels he hasn't yet won her, he tends to be great at focusing on her completely.

Equally amazing is the statement I occasionally hear from women that the best sex they ever have is the first time they go to bed with someone. This should never be true. Sex should become better and better, as you grow closer to each other. Your passion grows as you learn more about how to meet each other's needs. I'll go so far as to say that anybody who claims, "Sex is the best for me the first time," has never had a good relationship.

Notice, however, that I said this statement *should* never be true. Unfortunately it sometimes is true for some women. The only reason a woman could accurately make such a statement would be *if the "first time" were the only time a particular man was centering his full, undivided attention on her, and he subsequently allowed his focus to diminish.*

When men focus their complete attention on a woman during the stage of pursuit, they are behaving in a manner consistent with the age-old, and primarily male, activity of hunting. Simply put, the man places his total attention on her at that time because he's in active pursuit. In all too many cases, the minute he's "gotten" her, he doesn't feel he needs to pay attention anymore. Sad to say, some men are far better at getting what they want than at keeping it.

To those men who say they "don't know how" to pay attention to a woman, I say, "You can be sure of this: any man who is dating with any success, and has any romantic relationships that move into the stage of sexual intimacy, obviously knows how to pay attention to women." Maybe he is not continuing to pay attention, in order to make the relationship work during the conviction and the commitment stage, *but he knows how.*

In a good relationship, as it progresses, the woman should feel more and more certain that her happiness is a priority to her man and that he will give her attention.

But I'm not just talking about sex. Paying attention to a woman means truly noticing what's going on with her and acknowledging it in some loving manner—such as observing that she seems cold and getting up to get her a sweater, or perhaps adjusting the shade when you notice the sunlight is in her eyes. Often the little, everyday things can make her feel she's the center of your attention. The key is to *pay attention to her needs in and out of bed.*

Even a little bit of focused, concentrated attention will go a long way. You may say, "Well, I can't do it all the time." Of course you can't do it *all* the time. Just make sure you *do* it, and do it regularly. If you come home from work you may very well need some unwinding time—to watch TV, eat dinner, read the paper for a while—but just make sure that, at some point during the evening, you shift and focus your total attention on your woman. *Even if you only do this for an hour a day, have your focus completely on her.*

When you're focusing your complete attention on her, it means you don't read the newspaper while you're talking to her, you don't look at the TV; instead, *you really listen*. All that is important in your world at that moment is paying attention to your woman. Never forget she is *the* woman in your life, and she is the one who is going to make you happy—but only if you make her happy.

4. *To feel cherished*

To feel cherished is to know, from the depth of your being and beyond all doubt, that you are held dearly, that you are nurtured, that you are honored and revered. A woman needs to feel that she is cherished by her man, that he nurtures her, that he honors her, that he's proud to be with her.

How can a man demonstrate this to a woman? He might turn to her often and tell her how really lucky he feels to be with her. A woman needs to hear this, not once at the beginning of a relationship, but daily. *She must feel that you recognize her for the prize that she is*. And the magic that happens as a result is wonderful, for if you cherish her, she will become the greatest prize you've ever had. Cherish her and she will make you happy.

5. *To be listened to*

Observers in the field of gender relations have made an astounding discovery: *Men and women don't listen the same*. From John Gray to Deborah Tannen, authors are burning up the bestseller lists with books about the differences in male and female communication styles, and the problems these differences can cause.

There are few situations in which these differences are more apparent than when men and women discuss their problems with each other. When a man has a problem—for example, when he's had a terrible day at work—he wants to come home, retreat to his "cave" and sort out his problems on his own. He doesn't want to talk until he's figured out the solution, and what he wants from his woman then is reassurance that he's found (or will find) the *right* solution.

When a woman talks to a man about her problems, she's usually still in the process of finding a solution. She needs for him to just let her "outflow." Women communicate this way with each other all the time. *What a woman really needs is for a man to just listen to her with his total attention on what she's saying.* Let's say she's the one who's had the bad day at work and she starts to talk to her man. She wants to "empty out" and be reassured he is with her; she wants to be heard, to talk it out and have him be a sounding board as she is dealing with the situation. She wants empathy. But unless she specifically asks for a solution, she doesn't want him to step in and offer one.

Even when a woman is not talking about her problems, she still wants to be listened to with full attention and without constant interruptions. She wants to feel as if what she says matters to the man in her life.

There are some men—and they are truly remarkable creatures—who can get along with any woman. A man like this may fall short in every area of a relationship but this one: *he knows how to listen to a woman.* Granted, there's always a new woman in his life, because once a woman realizes that he doesn't meet her other needs, she moves on (or else he starts feeling pressure to give more, and *he* leaves). Yet he always finds himself surrounded by women, because he knows how to listen.

Can you see how important listening is? If a man learns only this one lesson, women will flock to him. I'm not claiming that listening will make your relationship perfect, but if you learn to listen to your woman with your full attention—and with empathy rather than the desire to offer a solution—you'll be fulfilling one of her most important needs in the relationship.

6. *Affection and romance*

I read in a study once that for a woman to be emotionally well-balanced, she needs to be touched ten to twelve times a day—not sexually but in a loving and tender way. Sex is very important to men. That's not to say it isn't important to women, but for women, affection is a necessary prerequisite to sex. If you men want to have a sexually fulfilled life, you have to be physically affectionate and demonstrative with the woman in your life. *You have to touch her a lot even when you're not in the bedroom.* If you want her to be ready tonight, you cannot simply say, "Are you in the mood?" If *you* haven't been affectionate, she's not going to be playful.

How can you make your woman feel she's getting romance and affection? Every woman has her own preferences. There are many ways a man can say, "I adore you"—flowers, small gifts, tender touches, spontaneous love notes, or all of the above. Learn what makes *her* feel special.

And always, always make her feel as if you think she's the most beautiful woman in the world. *Virtually any woman has a primary need to feel that she remains always beautiful to the man in her life, more beautiful to him than anyone else in the entire world.* I mentioned this earlier but it's worth repeating and elaborating upon.

One key to making a woman feel beautiful is to compliment her sincerely *and, above all, not criticize her.* Anyone can tell her that she is beautiful, and she may or may not believe it, but if the man in her life tells her that she needs to lose five pounds, she'll be devastated. Criticizing a woman's physical attractiveness is very dangerous to the well-being of the relationship; it is very much like criticizing a man's ability to produce (e.g., make money, excel in sports). A woman has to be very careful if she even makes a suggestion to a man about his ability to produce. In regard to a woman's physical attractiveness, a man has to be equally careful.

A woman I know, named Cathy, tells the incredible tale of an ex-boyfriend who once said to her, immediately after lovemaking, "I hope you realize that you've gained a couple of pounds recently." Needless to say, that put a damper on the afterglow and, for Cathy, on the entire relationship. She left her boyfriend soon after that and is now in a relationship with a man who makes her feel beautiful all the time.

What Cathy's boyfriend could have done, if he'd truly thought she "needed" to lose some weight, was to find some way of *positively* reinforcing her. He could have picked an appropriate time and said, "I think you've lost some weight. You look even better than usual; I don't know, even more sexy."

Whatever you do, don't ever come out and directly criticize a woman's physical appearance. If you do that, you're going to have a woman on your hands who does not want to have sex tonight *because she does not feel pretty*. (And if, like Cathy's boyfriend, you wait until *after* sex to drop your bombshell, you'll end up with a bitter partner who may never want to have sex with you again.)

So how often do you have to display affection and romance in order for your woman to feel fulfilled? In a word, *constantly*. You may be saying, "What? I have to constantly give her romance? I have to constantly tell her she's beautiful?" I will answer that question with another question: "How often do you want to have sex?" Constantly, right? Well, then I think you'd better make her feel beautiful. *Making her feel beautiful is not a one-time event, but an ongoing process*. If you want to keep having hot passionate sex, then romance and affection have to be there for your woman.

It's a trade-off. If you keep the romance and affection there, she'll keep a hot passionate sex life for you, filled with variety and spontaneity. It's a good trade, where both parties win.

7. For her man to totally embrace her goals

Where a man simply needs to feel that a woman admires him for his work, a woman actually needs the man in her life to embrace her goals, to truly support her, and to give her some definite encouragement.

Verbal encouragement is very important to a woman. If her goal is to be a fund-raiser for a charity, or to go back to college to get a degree, or to start her own business, tell her you think it's a great idea. Even if you think it's ridiculous, if it's her goal and it doesn't compromise your well-being, embrace it. (Besides, she might surprise you; it's amazing what women can do.) Of course you want to be realistic; but in general, encourage her, support her, be her best friend. Don't be critical, for she may take even "constructive" criticism as discouragement. Instead be positive by acknowledging her successes and triumphs. And above all, *never come across as condescending or patronizing in your support.*

HIS NEEDS

For a woman to have her needs fulfilled she needs the support of her man. Women, the best way to get this support is to be there for *him* when he needs you. So let's switch now and talk about men's top seven needs.

1. To feel adequate and okay just the way he is

This is a man's first and foremost need. He has to feel his woman accepts him and is not trying to control or change him. That's why, generally speaking, a woman must be supportive of her man in a very discreet way so that he doesn't feel she's controlling or interfering.

Males grow up being nurtured and taken care of by their mothers, but at some point they separate from their mothers and go off to become MEN. As such, society says *they're* supposed to be in charge. Though gender roles have become more equal, most men are programmed not to want a woman to see what they, as "grown men," perceive as weaknesses in themselves. Much less do they want a woman criticizing them or telling them what to do. *They have to feel they are okay just the way they are.*

For example, if a woman starts out by telling a man, "I don't like the way you dress," he's not going to feel terribly adequate. He may feel uncomfortable, embarrassed, or downright resentful of her. The wisest approach in this case is for her to just accept the way he dresses, but if she wants to subtly guide him in another fashion direction, she might buy him a little present that reflects her taste in clothes (though only when she feels it is the appropriate time in the relationship). If he starts to dress "better" after that, fine. If he doesn't take the hint, and this really bothers her, she needs to seriously reevaluate the relationship.

Women, the bottom line is this: Don't start out trying to change a man. If you haven't found a man you like the way he is, then you need to move on, because (1) you're *not* going to change him, and (2) he's not going to be happy with you.

2. *To feel he's in charge*

This might sound rather old-fashioned, but please hear me out. *Men have to believe they're in charge of their environment.*

Have you ever noticed a man when he goes on vacation? His first act upon reaching his destination is to look around. He wants to know how the hotel is laid out, where the ice machine is, where the nearest restaurants are. That's the way he reassures himself that he has his bearings. While he may believe his motives are purely pragmatic, in essence he wants to feel he's in charge.

The same happens with the remote control for the television set, and this phenomenon is a frequent theme in comedy routines. Though a man's constant channel-surfing may drive a woman to distraction, that remote is very symbolic to a man; holding it means he's in charge.

It's reasonable to assume that this desire to be in charge is another aspect of human male nature dating back to prehistoric times. Traditionally the male of our species has been the pursuer, the hunter; even today there are many ways a man plays out this role of a hunter pursuing his "kill."

Does that mean a woman should never make the first move? Absolutely not! She just has to do it with finesse. And, as the following story shows, you're never too young to learn this lesson.

Some time ago I was at a large dinner party in the banquet room of a fine restaurant. It was a party of adults, with the exception of two children: ten-year-old Nicole and eleven-year-old Jason. Nicole was surely one of the most precocious, outgoing ten-year-olds I've ever had the pleasure of knowing. Jason, on the other hand, was shy and quiet—very much at that awkward stage. Nicole was obviously interested in Jason and repeatedly made an effort to draw him into some sort of interaction. But for each attempt she made, he would become more withdrawn, blushing bright red, hiding his face in his hands, slumping into his chair and looking as if he desired nothing more than to vanish.

Nicole, however, would not give up. Jason's mother was seated beside the boy, and Nicole tugged on her sleeve, begging her to trade places with her at the table. Finally the mother whispered to Nicole, "Sweetheart, I think you're just going to have to give up for now. He's way too shy. He's at that age where he really doesn't know how to behave around girls."

I was seated nearby, watching this little scene and wondering what I could do to help. Two facts registered: one, the movie *Jurassic Park* was playing on the big-screen TV in an adjoining room, and two, I knew Jason was passionately interested in dinosaurs. I beckoned Nicole over and said to her, "Nicole, here's what I want you to try. Go over to Jason and whisper in his ear, 'Do you know anything about dinosaurs? And if you do, could you tell me a little about them . . . and do you think we could go in the other room and watch *Jurassic Park*?' "

Nicole immediately brightened, ran back over to Jason, and whispered into his ear. Let me tell you, the change in that boy was immediate and dramatic. In a matter of seconds he was transformed from an awkward little boy to a self-assured young man. He straightened up, rose from his seat, puffed out his chest, and offered his hand to Nicole. As he led her into the room where the movie was playing, he was talking her ear off. His mother was absolutely astonished; her mouth had fallen open and the color had drained from her face. She turned to me and said, "My God, what did you say to her?" I smiled and replied, "Well, that's a secret between Nicole and me." Several other people had also noticed the transformation and wanted to know what sort of magic I had worked. Then someone mentioned that I was a relationship expert and, though it had hardly been my intention, I sold a few tapes that night. At any rate, to everybody who was at that party: now you know what really happened between Jason and Nicole.

I like to think that this little incident marked the beginning of a fine friendship. The point is, whether the couple in question is ten, twenty, or forty years old, the woman may very well be the one who initiates the relationship—but there comes a time when she has to switch and make him feel *he's* pursuing *her*. She can give him signals that she's available, but in some way she has to make him believe he's in charge. You've no doubt heard the old saying, "He chased her till she caught him." That's a pretty accurate reflection of the way many couples begin their relationships.

During the course of the relationship most people find that the role of pursuer changes hands often. It changes many times all the way through the commitment stage (we'll talk about that more in chapter five), but the man must always be able to feel that, essentially, he's in charge of what's happening. He needs to feel he is making decisions for himself and that you're not making decisions for him.

3. *To be admired and respected*

A man absolutely must feel that his woman is *proud* of him, that when she looks at him she feels very lucky to be with him.

There's a difference between making a woman feel cherished and making a man feel admired. A man needs to feel looked up to. Again, that may seem somewhat old-fashioned, but what it basically means is that he needs to feel his woman values his advice. A woman can really score points with a man by asking him a question about something he knows. This will not only make him feel in charge, it will make him feel you admire him because you are seeking his advice.

A man must also feel that a woman is really glad she's with him. He must feel she's proud of him and proud of what he's done with his life. Every man needs to be acknowledged for his successes, whatever (or however humble) they may be. He wants the woman in his life to notice because she *is* the woman in his life. This brings us to another secret, one which some men may not be willing to admit: *only with a woman in his life can a man really feel like a man and feel completely validated.* Not even compliments from his male friends can give a man the same validation, the same surge of pride, that he receives when his woman praises him.

For a man to really feel admired and respected by his woman, she must show him she trusts that he is going to do the right thing. This doesn't mean she should refrain from giving advice when her man specifically asks for it from her. If he considers her his very best friend, he may frequently request advice from her. But she should give it tactfully, with an awareness of what the man is really requesting.

So many times, when a man asks a woman for advice, he's asking for more than advice; he's asking for reassurance that he will do the right thing. So a woman should always end her advice by letting him know *she believes whatever choice he makes will be the right choice.* This is another fine line: the woman must give him advice and, at the same time, make him feel that he is in charge, he is adequate, he is okay and she admires who he is. And even though she may have noticed something that he overlooked because he's not seeing things from her perspective, *she gives the criticism with such a subtle nuance that it's a suggestion, not a criticism.*

Since she is advising him as his best friend, she is reminding him that she admires him and that she knows even if she weren't there, he would be capable of handling it all on his own. *It's very important for a man to know that his woman feels he is capable without her.*

4. For a woman to be his confidante

This is a very critical need, directly related to some of the points we just made above. In order for a woman to be a man's confidante, he must feel he can trust her to listen to him and give him feedback.

This is important always, but particularly when he feels afraid, for that is the time when a man is most vulnerable. Let's say the man you love is a lawyer and he confesses to you that he's quite anxious about a trial that's coming up. His sharing this with you is very intimate because he's revealing a vulnerability. Your job is to listen to him and not make light of it. You cannot just say, "Well, act like a man. Go in there and you'll be fine." That's what any man would tell him. You're his woman, and he's coming to you for more substantial support than he can get from his male friends.

A much better approach is to say: "Yes, I understand. You know, I'm really afraid in my work when I have to get up and teach a class. When I'm in front of the room for the first time, I'm absolutely terrified. So, I understand what it must feel like to do what you're going to do, but I know that you're going to be fine. Just think about all the cases that you've won."

Give him encouragement. Let him know that he's in charge, but don't make light of his fears.

This points out a significant difference in the way men and women handle their friendships. Most men still feel uncomfortable going to other men, even their close friends, and saying, "I'm scared." Women take it for granted that they can share such emotions with their female friends. A woman can call her girlfriend on the telephone and say, "My God, I'm having a horrible day. I feel so sad [or scared, or fat, or ugly]." But it's still not "okay" for a man to call up his friends and complain, "Boy, I feel like a loser. I'm scared to death to get up in front of that jury, afraid everyone will see how inadequate I really am."

Men are competitive, by nature or nurture or a combination thereof. They share experiences together, such as sports; when they get together, it's usually for a specific activity, even if it's just watching football on TV. While it's true that more and more men these days are trying to develop relationships where they share their innermost feelings with each other, so far only the most enlightened men do this.

The only place a man really has a true confidante with whom to share his fears, his secrets, his insecurities, is with the woman in his life. She must realize what a sacred trust he has bestowed upon her. Besides giving him encouragement and never making light of the fears he expresses, above all, she must *never* talk about his concerns to others or in front of others. That means she doesn't talk about them even to her best girlfriend, or her sister, or her mother. *These are his secrets.* Yet you might be surprised how many women don't realize this. A man has to feel that he can trust his woman. If she does not live up to this important role as his best friend and probably his only confidante, he'll never be completely satisfied in his relationship with her.

5. *Companionship*

A man wants the woman in his life to not only be a sexy creature who makes him feel wonderful when he walks in a room with her—because she's attractive to look at, and she openly admires him—but *he also wants her to have fun with him.*

What this means is that she has to embrace at least some of his recreational needs and some of his interests. This doesn't mean a woman has to do everything the man does. Couples need time apart, and they need to have other friends. But there are many ways a couple can have fun together—whether it's dancing, movies, playing tennis, exercise, shopping, listening to music, or reading and discussing books.

Women, remember that your man looks to you for relief from the pressure of work. He wants a playmate, and I don't mean the centerfold type. He wants someone with whom he can have fun, someone who's a good time, somebody with whom he can laugh and truly enjoy himself. So you must be a good recreational companion for him.

6. *To feel appreciated*

A man will not be happy feeling admired just for what he does. He has to feel that his woman appreciates what he does *for her*. If he's romantic with her, if he leaves her little love notes, she has to let him know that she really appreciates it. When he tells her she's beautiful, she lets him know how much it means to hear him tell her. She lets him know how lucky she feels, how rare it is to have a man who makes his woman feel so pretty. When he makes a trip to the grocery store to get something for her when she's ill, she lets him know how special it makes her feel—if not immediately, then perhaps the next day when she's feeling better.

Above all a man must never feel taken for granted. The quickest way to get a man to do nothing is to fail to appreciate him. If a woman doesn't appreciate him long enough—and she criticizes him enough—he will shut down completely and won't do a thing. That doesn't mean a woman needs to be a sycophant. She just needs to be appreciative.

7. *To feel sexually fulfilled*

Just because it's the seventh and the last certainly does not mean that this is the least important. On the contrary, *men need sexual satisfaction to feel like men.* They have to have sex to feel they're complete.

Here's something else that not all women know: *As much as he needs to experience his own orgasm, a man also needs to feel he is satisfying his woman and giving her an orgasm.* In a later chapter we'll go into detail about desire and sex, but beyond the mechanics and techniques, women must realize that a man needs to feel sexually satisfied.

Obviously, a woman isn't going to want to have sex with someone who isn't satisfying her romantic needs, her need for affection, and her need to feel beautiful. By the same token, a man is not going to want to meet *her* needs if his sexual needs aren't met. You have to be available and physically responsive as his sexual partner.

All of these seven needs of women, and all seven needs of men, are very important—which means that in some way, all seven of them have to be met in order for a relationship to be successful.

A woman, for example, can't "drop the ball" in any area and expect her man to be completely satisfied. She can admire the work he does, but if she doesn't appreciate the little things he does for *her*, he's not going to feel completely content and completely satisfied.

Similarly, a man may make his woman feel beautiful, but if he doesn't make her feel secure, or feel like the top priority in his life, she's not going to be completely fulfilled in the relationship. If the need to feel beautiful is important enough to her she may remain in this incomplete relationship for a long time, even if none of her other needs are being met. Believe it or not, I have seen women hang on for years simply because they were with a man who could make them feel beautiful. These women may have felt beautiful, but were they happy? Were they content? No, they weren't. They were merely able to cover their unhappiness with the fact that their one overwhelming hunger was met. That is a very poor substitute for a real, loving relationship. Unfortunately, it is all too common.

To summarize:

WHAT A WOMAN NEEDS IN A RELATIONSHIP . . .

1. SECURITY (EMOTIONAL)
2. TO FEEL THAT SHE IS NUMBER ONE IN HER MAN'S LIFE
3. ATTENTION (FOCUS ON HER)
4. TO FEEL CHERISHED
5. TO BE LISTENED TO
6. AFFECTION AND ROMANCE
7. FOR HER MAN TO TOTALLY EMBRACE HER GOALS

WHAT A MAN NEEDS IN A RELATIONSHIP . . .

1. TO FEEL ADEQUATE JUST THE WAY HE IS
2. TO FEEL HE'S IN CHARGE
3. TO BE ADMIRED AND RESPECTED
4. TO HAVE HIS WOMAN AS HIS CONFIDANTE
5. COMPANIONSHIP
6. TO FEEL APPRECIATED
7. TO FEEL SEXUALLY FULFILLED

♥ ♥ ♥

Before we talk about the three major relationship needs that are common to both men and women, I have a simple assignment for you. It's time to take out your Relationship Journal again (if you don't want to write in the spaces provided in this book). As you did for the exercises in the first chapter, think carefully about your answers. Take as much time, and use as much paper, as you need.

DETERMINING YOUR NEEDS, AND HOW YOUR PARTNER CAN MEET THEM

For the first part of this exercise you're going to write down your needs. In your own private space, with no input from anyone else, write what would make you feel that all of your needs were being met. If you're a woman, go back and look at the list of the seven top needs of women. Write the ways in which *each* of these needs could be met for you. If you're a man, refer to the men's list and do the same.

In chapter one we said, "Everything begins with knowing what you want." That also applies to the needs we've talked about in this chapter. Even though the basic relationship needs may be the same for most men or for most women, the ways in which these needs can be met vary with each individual.

After all, you're a person, not a box that comes with written directions. We're all unique; we have to know what makes us happy, and we have to be able to explain this to our partner. It's important that you be completely clear and very specific about what *you* need.

♥ ♥ ♥ ♥ ♥ ♥ ♡ ♥ ♥ ♥ ♥ ♥ ♥

EXERCISE 2-1.
MY PARTICULAR NEEDS AS A MAN/WOMAN ARE:

Need	*How it can be met for me*
1.	
2.	
3.	
4.	
5.	
6.	
7.	

DETERMINING YOUR PARTNER'S NEEDS, AND HOW YOU CAN MEET THEM

Now it's time to make a second list. This is a list of what you believe to be the other person's needs, and what you think might work to fulfill those needs.

It is important to do this exercise even if you are not yet in a relationship. Once you do get into that relationship, of course, you're going to get more feedback on what's really right for that unique person—but for now, just think in general terms, e.g.: "How do I make a man or a woman happy?" "What are some of the things that I could do to meet his or her needs?"

Think of this as preparation. From the moment the relationship starts, from the moment your eyes meet across the room and you start to talk, the time clock starts running. These needs start coming into play right away. The woman wants to know, "Does he think I'm beautiful?" The man wants to know, "Does she think I'm okay just the way I am? Does she admire me?"

At this early stage, the ways in which the respective needs are met can be as simple as the man saying, "That dress really brings out the color of your eyes," or the woman saying, "I love the tie you have on tonight."

How well you meet the other person's needs (and how well *your* needs are met) will determine how far this relationship is going to go. *If you don't start meeting these needs early, you may never get another opportunity.*

♥ ♥ ♥ ♥ ♥ ♡ ♥ ♥ ♥ ♥ ♥ ♥ ♥

EXERCISE 2-2. MY PARTNER'S NEEDS AS A MAN/WOMAN ARE:

Need	*How I can meet that need*
1.	
2.	
3.	
4.	
5.	
6.	
7.	

Before we close this chapter, let's explore the Big Three: the three basic relationship needs that are common to men and women.

THE THREE COMMON NEEDS

Men and women are different in so many ways, but in some very basic ways we're remarkably the same. There are three common needs we all have in a relationship. These ingredients are so important that without them a relationship simply will not work.

1. ***Trust.*** You cannot possibly expect to be happy in a relationship with a person you don't trust. Trust is an essential ingredient to a happy relationship. But it's a two-way street: each person has to be trusted *and* trustworthy.
2. ***Respect.*** If you lose, or never have, respect for your mate and his/her value system, your relationship will not last.
3. ***Like.*** Forget the passion, forget the lust—well, okay, maybe you can't exactly forget them, but do know that in order for a relationship to work, this person has to be someone you really like to be with, whom you'd have fun with, and whom you'd spend time with even if you *weren't* attracted sexually, if there were no chemistry at all. For a relationship to succeed, you have to really enjoy being with that person. If the relationship is based merely on chemistry, you can be sure the chemistry will ultimately go away—and you may be left with a nightmare.

I hope, by now, that you understand a little more about what it takes to give you contentment in a relationship, and what it may take for you to make your potential partner content. Now you're ready to go a step further, to the third principle, *Connecting.*

♥ The Third Principle ♥

CONNECTING

Before you can begin to build a relationship with another person, that person must have the desire to enter into the process with you. You may be a perfect match for each other, but if you don't start connecting—establishing a link or bond with the person—from the very beginning, you'll never find out.

The first two principles we discussed were really laying the ground rules. You've set the stage for what you want and need. You have established a process for communicating those needs to your partner. It's like taking dancing lessons; you've learned the steps, you've picked the music you like. You've even decided whom you want to dance with. Now it's time to *act*. You've got to get the person to want to dance with *you*. The music is playing, so let's begin. . . .

This is a topic that has been covered many times before. So many books and articles have been written about how to attract someone. Though some of this material contains some pretty good ideas, I can't help but wonder: why isn't all that advice working? With all the books and tapes out there, why don't we *all* know how to instantly get someone? Why are so many wonderful, delightful people still looking, always looking, yet never finding the person they want?

My purpose here is to share with you not merely good ideas, but *actual techniques* that have worked well for many people—including people with much less going for them than you have. I'm not going to teach you how to flirt, how to seduce, or how to come up with a great opening line. I do hope to show you how to ***truly connect with other people,*** how to attract people into your life who can participate in your future growth.

But first I think we'd better say a few words on how *not* to connect.

FLIRTING WITH TROUBLE?

Many people think flirting is a harmless pastime. But is it? As a matter of fact, flirting can keep you from truly connecting with someone.

Most of the people I know who have good, long-term relationships are not flirtatious at all. They are very much one-man women and one-woman men. They are, however, friendly people who have a knack for *connecting* with everybody.

Take Stacy, a friend of mine who, prior to her engagement, dated many men. She's always been very popular, has had several successful relationships, and, in fact, has received more marriage proposals than any woman I've ever known. One day I said to her, "Stacy, I want to talk to you about getting people's attention, and about attracting men. What do you think about flirting?"

Stacy replied, "*I've* never been a flirt. Have you ever seen me be seductive, bat my eyes, or in any way act flirtatious with a man other than the one I'm with? I'm a very faithful, very loyal person."

We were in the grocery store at this time, and as we approached the checkout lane a male sacker recognized Stacy and rushed up to her, took her cart, and whisked her into a line ahead of several other people. Stacy greeted the checker with a smile and then said to her sacker friend, "So how are you doing today, Alex? It's a beautiful day, isn't it?"

He said, "Yes, it is. It's really pretty." They continued their light banter as he sacked her groceries, and then he eagerly said, "Here, let me take your key and get you out to your car."

As we exited the store she asked him, "By the way, are you still playing those lotteries?" He said, "Yes. I even had one win." Stacy replied with genuine enthusiasm, "Oh, really? That's great. Do you have a system?" With that he launched into an enthusiastic recounting of his personal lottery number-picking system.

Throughout this exchange I noticed how well Stacy connected with this person. She wasn't flirting, and she certainly wasn't attempting to seduce him; she was *connecting*.

The dictionary's definition of "flirt" is "to act amorously . . .

without serious intention." This certainly doesn't sound like something a person of integrity would do. To "seduce," according to the same dictionary, means to persuade someone to have sexual intercourse with you for the first time. It also means "to lead astray from duty, to persuade someone into wrongdoing by offering temptations."

Well, who would want to persuade someone to do something they didn't want to do, or that wasn't good for them? Who would want to act with such false intentions? Is this the type of person you want to be, or want to have a relationship with?

Women, when you're flirting with a man across the room and acting seductively toward him, what is he thinking about? Is he thinking about you as a person? Is he thinking about getting to know you, or about having a serious relationship in the future with you? No! He is responding to the *seduction*, not the person. In other words, he is focusing on sex. At this point, a relationship does exist, but it is a shallow one at best. It may result in sex, but sex in and of itself does not equal intimacy.

Or, men, think about this. A woman is batting her eyes, essentially using you for an "equipment check"—gauging your responses to make sure her seductive apparatus is still in working order. Is she thinking about you as a person? Is she thinking about advancing her (or your) spiritual growth? No, she's not. She's looking to you for validation of her attractiveness.

I'm assuming you want to attract your soul mate, someone with whom to spend your life. You cannot do this by being deceptive or by "acting in an amorous way without serious intention." You can't do it by trying to persuade someone to have sex with you when you don't have any intention of becoming emotionally involved with that person.

ELEVEN SECRETS TO MAKING A TRUE CONNECTION

You may be wondering what I mean by "connection," if *not* that initial surge of excitement you feel when some incredibly attractive person first catches your eye. That's a fair question, so let me explain. By connection, I mean *that initial link with a person and the sense that there is, at some level, an affinity between the two of you.* That link is a signpost that herein lie the makings of a real relationship.

Before we go any further I want to share a list of eleven secrets about connecting. These are all important to know if you truly want to connect with someone, *anyone*; in fact, I recommend you use them to enhance all of the relationships in your life, not just the relationship with your soul mate.

1. Your happiness depends on you and your state of mind—not on your state of matrimony or relationship. Think of this secret as the Prime Directive. *You don't have to be married, or in a relationship, to be happy.* Happiness, like self-confidence, is an inside job. In fact, let's face it: there are many unhappy married people out there. They're miserable and wish they were single. They think single people have it all. While it's fine to set a goal of having a wonderful, loving relationship, it is a mistake to believe that you can't be happy until you reach that goal. *You've got to enjoy the journey.* You have to *live* your joy, not search for it.

2. You cannot be too attached to the outcome of the relationship. If you can accept the first secret, this one shouldn't be too difficult. In chapter one we talked a little bit about the importance of not getting too attached, but it's a point worth repeating because it is absolutely critical to remember when you're contemplating a relationship with anybody.

I want to make an important distinction here. Remaining unattached to the outcome doesn't mean that you don't *care* about the person or the relationship. It means that you don't have a clearly defined script which must be followed in order for you to realize a positive benefit from your involvement. Your goal is to attract people and connect with them, as opposed to attaching yourself to some specific result.

Please note this secret applies at any stage of a relationship, not only at the beginning. Technically, a relationship exists from the moment you meet somebody. Whether it becomes a lifelong relationship or merely lasts a few hours, you should gaze "with hunter's eye," as a poet once wrote, to constantly seek its value to your continued growth and happiness.

3. Two whole people make a relationship work, not two desperate people trying to fill up their own emptiness with someone else. You do not want to attach yourself to another person out of desperation, hoping to reinforce your sense of self-worth. Even as you do not want to be attached to an outcome, you don't want to be attached to another person in such a way as to restrict the person's freedom to grow. Your objective is to connect, to link with people who are going to help you along your path to being a better person.

Men, do you think that a woman can't tell if you are in desperate need of attaching yourself to her? Women, do you think that men can't tell if you're looking for a meal ticket or someone to take care of you?

No one wants a person who is, as one friend of mine put it, "a black hole of human need." You want a whole, vibrant, unique person who has a full life. *You want to be with someone who brings happiness* ***into*** *a relationship, not someone who desperately looks to the relationship as his or her sole source of happiness.*

4. People want to connect with a happy, confident person. One of the biggest turn-ons in the world is a person who is obviously happy. Everybody wants to be around a happy person. When happy people walk in the room, smiling and upbeat, people gravitate toward them because they want to share that person's happiness and confidence. Just by being around a happy person, others begin to see the same happy world for themselves.

How, then, do you realize your own happiness and confidence, so you can project it to others? A great way to start is to go back to the exercises you did for the first chapter and concentrate on what is good about you. Focus on your assets and on how you're diminishing your liabilities. Don't forget to look at that little list and the affirmation you created to carry around with you everywhere. *Do whatever it takes to reinforce your confidence in yourself.*

Remind yourself that you are a unique, worthwhile person. Build your confidence, and make sure that confidence comes across every time you encounter another person.

5. *Smile, smile, smile! Learn the art of the genuine smile, and practice it often.* This goes along with happiness and confidence. Perhaps you feel this advice is simplistic, but think about it—what do happy, confident people consistently do? That's right: they *smile*. I'm not talking about a phony smile or a grimace, but a smile that comes from within. If you're working to develop and enforce your happiness and self-confidence, a genuine smile will come easily. So do learn to smile more—not just *at* people, but *within* yourself. You'll be amazed at the difference it makes. As the old song says, "Smile, and the world smiles with you."

6. *Practice eye contact—but don't overdo it.* It has been truthfully said that the eyes are the windows to the soul. People *want* you to look at them. And people who want to establish a level of intimacy with you want you to look beyond their surface.

They also want to know that you are looking in and focusing on *them and only them*, not on everything else that's going on in the room. There's nothing worse for a woman than being on a date and having the guy sit there looking around the room at all the other women who walk in. What does this say to her? It says that this man's interest in her will last only until something better comes along. *People who are good connectors make eye contact, and place their focus entirely on the person they're trying to connect with.* Making eye contact with a person helps keep that person's focus on you as well.

This eye-contact business can be a bit of a double-edged sword, however, and should be handled somewhat delicately. While you want to establish good eye contact to let a person know you are interested, you don't want to stare unceasingly into the person's eyes. Look away occasionally, to think about what has been said and to allow each of you a sense of private space. While intimacy involves sharing each other's secrets, we all need to feel that part of us is withheld from general view.

You probably know what it feels like to have someone gaze intently into your eyes, never looking away. You sometimes get the feeling that you're in the company of one of those emotional "black holes" we mentioned earlier—that the person wants to fill up with *your* thoughts and feelings. Or perhaps you feel the person is trying in some way to manipulate you, exercise some sort of control, establish some type of power over you, with an unwavering gaze. In any case, you don't like it, and neither does anybody else.

No matter how deep the level of intimacy you achieve with another person, you each need to maintain your own individual space, inviolate. When you first meet someone, it's particularly important to respect the boundaries of individual space. Master the judicious use of eye contact, and you've gone a long way toward mastering the art of connecting.

7. Genuinely care and have empathy for the other person. We all need to feel that someone really cares about us. When you go to a therapist, you pay one hundred dollars or more an hour for the privilege of having the therapist listen to you with great focus. She may ask a few questions to help you think about your situation from a different perspective, but for the most part she simply listens. And generally, you leave feeling better. I have a friend who refers to therapy as "rent-a-friend." But no matter what we think about it, the truth is that it helps. In fact, I think it would help if the counselor didn't give you any advice at all. What she's giving you of value is her total focus, her energy. Your self-esteem goes up because you're feeling a connection with another human being.

What happens if you go to regular sessions with a therapist for a year? At the end of that year, you may know virtually nothing about the therapist, but you feel very close to her because she knows so much about *you*. The key to connection here is not so much that you're telling all about yourself and sharing mystical clues about your innermost workings. It's that you're being focused on by someone who is genuinely interested in you.

Most of our relationships, of course, take place outside of the therapist's office. I have a good friend named Leah who, like my friend Stacy, connects with everyone. She connects with the saleswomen in department stores, with the waiters and waitresses in restaurants, with virtually everybody with whom she comes in contact—but she never flirts. She has a husband with whom she's madly in love, but men and women like her and remember her because she *connects*. Perhaps her greatest quality is that she's very empathetic. She genuinely *cares* about what people have to say, and they love her for it.

I suggest you cultivate this quality, too, but it must be as genuine as Leah's. In fact, this is a characteristic you don't even want to consider faking. You know how easy it is to spot someone who pretends to care about you when they really don't, and you know how uncomfortable you feel around someone like that.

You may be asking, "Okay, so how can I *create* a feeling of genuine caring? That almost seems a contradiction in terms." The truth is, it's really pretty simple: you have to have *empathy*. And empathy is something you can develop. How? You have to find something about the other person's situation or personality to which you can relate. Perhaps you can remember a time when you felt a similar emotion or had a similar experience. You need to figuratively walk in that person's shoes. As you begin to empathize, you will find you don't need to create or fake that caring. It will arise naturally.

Perhaps most important of all, learn to be a good listener. If eye contact and smiling are the icing, the art of *listening with your full attention* is the cake. If you really want to connect with somebody, ask questions that show you're truly interested in what that person thinks and feels.

8. Learn to laugh and find humor in your life. Once, when I was very ill, I read *Anatomy of an Illness* by Norman Cousins, in which he describes laughter as one of the greatest cures for illness. He helped heal himself by watching funny movies.

Cousins wasn't the first to discover that laughter and humor are important, and he certainly wasn't the last. Why do you think so many "humor consultants" are now making a living conducting seminars and workshops on how people can integrate laughter into their businesses and their personal lives? A whole new industry has grown up around the principle that laughter is vital to our well-being.

This doesn't mean that you have to be a professional comedian with a full repertoire of clever jokes. I'm not talking about *performing* humor; I'm talking about *recognizing* it and making it part of your life. It's crucial that you be capable of seeing humor in your life, even in yourself, and that you not be afraid to laugh at it. What a delightful experience it is to genuinely laugh, not *at* someone or something, but *with* them. When you develop your sense of humor, you develop your sense of joy in life.

Here's something else about laughter that you may not realize: *It's one of the greatest aphrodisiacs in the world.* Laughter and a smile can be more of a turn-on than bulging biceps or a low-cut blouse.

9. People like to be around other people who are like them; find something you have in common with the other person and tell that person. People who are skilled in the art of connecting know how to find common ground with virtually anybody. If you're talking to someone who expresses an interest in a topic that interests you, by all means, let the person know! This comes easily if you allow it, for more than likely the other person will be giving you all sorts of clues. It's your job to let someone know when he or she has mentioned something that sparks your interest.

So effective is this approach that there is even a sales technique called "match and marry," in which you zero in on something you have in common with your prospect and respond accordingly. By stepping on common ground with that person, you both feel more connected immediately.

There's only one catch, and you've probably guessed it: this common ground, like empathy, has to be genuine. You wouldn't want to fake it, anyway. If you have to *pretend* to relate to each other, the entire relationship will be built upon deception. Even if it did last longer than a few days, would you really want it to?

A fundamental requirement of a good relationship, and one of the factors that deepens the connection between two people, is the sense that the other person can contribute to your personal growth by providing you with new information or a fresh perspective. We're not talking about latching on to another person to "fill the hole in your soul." We're talking about connecting with someone who shares your interests and passions, and possesses knowledge that you believe will broaden *your* scope of knowledge and awareness.

A client of mine named Tammy has recently been thinking seriously about studying one of the forms of martial arts. She told me, "You wouldn't believe how many martial arts enthusiasts have 'magically' started to appear in my life, when I'd never encountered any before! In just two weeks, I've met at least three people who are taking different forms of martial arts. Of course, each of them believes that his or her particular form is the *only* proper one to learn. When I say I'm interested and that I'm trying to decide which form to study, they invariably launch into an explanation of why theirs is the very best. I listen intently because I truly am interested. And I really think each one of those people leaves liking me a little better."

I think Tammy's right. Her martial arts friends do leave liking her a little better because they've shared something of themselves with her and they feel connected to her. They feel that they are contributing to her life, that they are important and valuable to her. "And it's a two-way street," Tammy adds. "I leave feeling enriched by what they have shared, because they truly *have* contributed to my life."

In short, Tammy is connecting with these people.

10. Find something positive that you really like about a person and share it with them; if you genuinely like someone they almost always like you back. Always look for one positive thing that you really admire about a person, and let them know it. Of course, it must be genuine. Empty compliments always seem patronizing or manipulative. *Never, never, never pay a compliment you don't mean.*

Your compliment should be directed more to the person's substance than to physical attributes. For example, if you are trying to connect with someone who has a beautiful body, it's far more effective to say, "I admire the discipline it must take to work out and be in such great shape," than to simply say, "Wow, you have a gorgeous body." Put yourself in the other person's place: even if you do have a fantastic body, wouldn't you rather be admired for your self-discipline than your genetic good fortune? Wouldn't you rather hear praise about something for which you can take full credit?

11. Be approachable; no matter how attractive you are, you must be out there connecting with people. People don't connect with people who look unapproachable. No matter how beautiful or how handsome you are, if you don't smile, don't make eye contact, don't laugh, and generally don't seem interested, you won't connect. If you appear aloof, and uninterested in being approached, *nobody ever will approach you*, and you will never make a true connection with another person.

I found this out while working with clients of my video dating service. Some of the most glamorous women, who looked as if they had just stepped off a cover of *Vogue*, never got selected. On the other hand, the women who looked like the girl next door with the big smile were selected so many times we couldn't keep up with them. Why? Because they looked *approachable*.

If you think about it, you will see that all of the "secrets" on this list have one common element: they arise naturally when you allow them to. You don't have to *create* interest in, or focus upon, or caring for, someone you already find interesting and appealing. You don't have to force yourself to look at someone whom you find attractive. You just have to allow yourself to do what comes most naturally when you are enjoying the process and not obsessing about the end result.

GET OUT THERE AND PRACTICE!

Now that you have these secrets, the best way to use them is to *practice* them. That's what your assignment is for this chapter.

In your Relationship Journal or in the space I've provided,

make a note of three different people with whom you've decided you truly want to connect. The one stipulation is that you don't begin with some attractive person you spot across the room at a party or a club. It's best to start out slowly, in a situation where you don't feel you have so much at stake. In fact none of these people should be someone with whom you have had or want to have a romantic encounter. Here are my suggestions:

1. The first person should be a very casual acquaintance or perhaps someone whom you don't know at all.
2. The second person should be someone you work with, ideally, somebody with whom you do not get along very well.
3. The third person should be a platonic friend.

For example, try exerting your happiness with the sacker at the grocery store or the counter person at your favorite fast-food restaurant. Find out, in a safe situation, just how infectious and engaging your smile really is. As the person responds in kind, notice how much higher your confidence level is. This simple act will build your confidence much more than going out and catching someone's eye at a bar, batting your eyes, and wiggling seductively (or strutting defiantly if you're a man). The response your smile will elicit will be one of acknowledgment and appreciation.

As in previous chapters, *please do not skip over this assignment.* Truly practice being open, listening, being empathetic, and being generally better at connecting.

Gauge your progress; make notes each evening about what you did well and what you could have done better. If you really practice these techniques you will notice that people are connecting more easily with you, and getting more interested in you. This will help you tremendously when you begin dating.

You may begin this assignment right away, and complete it over the next week or so. Even after the assignment is completed, continue using the secrets of connecting with everyone you meet.

♥ ♥ ♥ ♥ ♡ ♥ ♥ ♥ ♥ ♥ ♥ ♥ ♥

Exercise 3-1. Practicing Connection Skills

Person Number 1: Casual acquaintance

Relationship: ____________________

Results:

____

____

____

____

Person Number 2: Coworker (with whom I am having conflict)

Relationship: ____________________

Results:

____

____

____

____

Person Number 3: Platonic friend

Relationship: ______________________________

Results:

____

____

____

____

OKAY, SO WHERE AND HOW DO I START MEETING THOSE WONDERFUL PEOPLE I'M ACTUALLY GOING TO DATE?

Let's say you're on your way to mastering the secrets of truly connecting with casual acquaintances and platonic friends. That's terrific. Sooner or later, however, you're going to want to start connecting with people for dating purposes. Where do you go to meet these people?

I'm not going to spend a great deal of time in this chapter on all the different ways you can meet people, because there are already plenty of books about that. The fact is you meet people everywhere—in the grocery store, while pursuing your hobbies, in classes, at the gym. *Meeting* people is the easy part; actually *connecting* with them is trickier.

Perhaps I'm prejudiced, but I think that video dating is a wonderful idea. You can be reasonably certain that the other people are really interested in relationships if they're willing to spend time, energy, and even some money to find people who interest them and screen out those who don't.

In my opinion, bars and clubs are some of the *poorest* places to meet interesting people. All too often, you end up with people who perceive drinking as a necessary tool for establishing relationships. And there's no doubt that some of these people have serious drinking problems. It's a hard place to make a significant soulful connection. I'm not saying you should completely eliminate clubs as a source of contact. Just be wary; be really awake, and very clear. Know your own limits, and stay within them. It's possible to meet the person of your dreams while partying at a club, but be clear enough (yes, I mean *sober* enough!) to tell the difference between the *person of your dreams* and the dreams themselves. You may have heard the old joke about "leaving the bar with a ten, but waking up with a two." It's a joke based in sad truth. Let the connection between you be real, based upon who you both are as people, not upon your comparative levels of need and intoxication. On that note, I'll put my soapbox away, at least until chapter four when we talk about safe sex.

Friends are a good source of people to meet. If you clearly state what you are looking for, your friends can be a wealth of material for relationships. You must, however, never assume that your friends know what you want.

Robin, a client I recently worked with, had ended a long-term relationship and decided she was ready to start dating again. When she asked me for advice, my first suggestion was that she try asking friends to introduce her to somebody. She returned a couple of weeks later, somewhat discouraged. "I've called up all my friends and asked them to introduce me to someone," Robin said. "They all told me the same thing: 'I don't know anyone who's good enough for you.' " Her friends' flattery was sincere; Robin happens to be a very attractive woman with a lot to offer—but all the compliments in the world couldn't bring her any closer to meeting somebody she wanted to date. "What should I do?" she asked me.

I suggested she try again but that she be more clear with her friends about how important this was to her. "Let them off the hook," I suggested. "Call them back and tell them to really think about it, but let them know you're not looking for a soul mate at this point. Your objective is just to start getting out again."

So Robin approached her friends a second time with clearer criteria. "I told them, 'Look, it doesn't have to be the person of my dreams; I just need to get out and start being around people again. I'm not looking for someone who meets impossibly high standards. I mean . . . do you know anyone who can breathe and walk at the same time?' "

Once she began placing more emphasis on the matter, once she let them know she was serious, her friends began to seriously consider her request. Then Robin decided to carry her plan a step further. "One of my closest friends, a woman named Sherri, owns a barbershop," she explained, "which means she cut lots of men's hair. To drive the point home about how serious I was, I said, 'Listen, Sherri, if you introduce me to someone I go out with more than three times, I'll give you two hundred dollars. If you introduce me to someone whom I actually have an intimate relationship with, I'll give you five hundred dollars.' Sherri laughed and laughed—until I said, 'I'm dead serious.'

"Sherri came up with a couple of candidates, each of whom I *did* go out with more than three times. When I offered to give her the money, she said, 'Don't be silly, you're one of my very closest friends.' The point is, offering the money made her realize how serious I was. It made her know I really wanted to meet people." In fact, Robin has been steadily dating one of the men Sherri introduced her to; they've been going out for a few months now and are planning a ski trip together.

I'm not suggesting that you adopt Robin's tactic of offering money, but you do have to let your friends know how important this is to you. And once they start fixing you up, thank them for it.

I hope I've got the wheels turning in your head. I hope you're realizing that you have lots of places to meet people; perhaps you're going to join a video dating service, or ask your friends to introduce you to someone, or scope out the possibilities at the gym or the community college where you take your night courses. There really are many choices, and we've just skimmed the possibilities here.

The best way to ensure that you actually start meeting people, however, is to set this up as a goal. The goal-setting principles we discussed in chapter one apply here too. All you have to do is set up a goal and write it down, e.g., *"I am going to meet and go out with at least two new people in the next thirty days.*" Then take steps to make that goal happen. Work at it just the way you would work at going out and finding prospects if you were in sales. The people you meet do not have to be the "perfect people"—the point is to get out there and get started.

NOW THAT I'M MEETING PEOPLE . . . WHAT IF THEY'RE NOT QUITE WHAT I EXPECTED?

Let's say you've set your goals and you've succeeded in making a date with someone; your best friend has fixed you up with a co-worker, or you've gone to a video dating service and chosen someone who looks promising. You're excited, perhaps a bit nervous, and you can't wait to practice the principles of connecting with this dream date.

What if the man or woman who shows up at the door or meets you after work at the local cappuccino bar is *not* the person of your dreams? First of all, even if you know right away that this is not your soul mate, or even someone you'll want to date casually, *you still want to connect with that person.* You don't need to go out again, but you do need to connect.

And just because this person wasn't the paragon you were hoping for, that doesn't mean you're going to have a miserable night. He or she may ultimately introduce you to your soul mate. Or this perfect stranger could become a dear friend, and you must never underestimate the value of a friend of the opposite sex. You just never know; everyone you meet is the key to a world of possibilities. Someone once said that each stranger is a bearer of gifts. I've found that to be true: every person has something unique to offer, but if you're so focused on what someone is not, you never will discover who that person *is*.

Above all, don't ever show disappointment. This is another human being, a person with feelings—so do everything you would normally do to connect with someone. You're not flirting, you're not trying to be seductive, you're not giving off false signals; you're trying to get to know your date as a person.

Don't be discouraged if the first *several* people you meet don't turn out to be potential soul mates. There is something in all of us that wants, even expects, instant gratification of our wishes; when we first start getting ourselves back out there in the world we only want to go out with "prime candidates."

It's a given that you're not going to meet your mate if you don't get out there, but if you haven't dated for a long time, or have been dating unsuccessfully, the odds are *you'd sabotage the relationship even if the perfect person walked through your door right now.* You need some people to "practice" with. You need people to sharpen your connecting skills with. In other words, you need those people who "aren't quite right" for you. If you truly practice finding what's good about everyone you meet, I can guarantee that you'll be richly rewarded.

THE THREE MODES OF ATTRACTION

We all use our various senses to process information from the world around us, but different people process in different ways. The science of Neuro-Linguistic Programming (NLP) teaches us that some people are predominantly *visual*, some are *auditory*, and some are *tactile*. While this is not the forum in which to explore NLP theory in detail, knowing about these different modalities can help us understand the dynamics of attraction. Very simply, there are three basic ways in which men and women may be attracted to each other:

1. ***Visual:*** Being attracted to the way somebody *looks*. (By the way, even though we've said again and again that men are visual, this doesn't mean *all* men are solely visual. Nor does it mean that no women are attracted to men on a visual basis.)
2. ***Auditory:*** Being turned on by a person's voice and what the person *says*—compliments, encouragement, etc.
3. ***Kinesthetic:*** Being warmed or turned on by someone's *touch*.

You probably fall into one of the above categories. Even so, your mode of attraction may vary depending on the person you're with. For example, you may meet somebody and be strongly attracted by the person's good looks. On another occasion, you may meet someone and be immediately smitten by that person's voice. Learn to pay attention to your patterns of attraction, and those of the people with whom you're trying to connect.

THE FIRST FEW DATES: A SURVIVAL GUIDE

I cannot overstress the importance of the first few dates in setting the tone of a relationship. Generally speaking, *a person decides within the first three dates whether or not this is someone with whom to pursue a relationship.* Both men and women make that crucial decision during this time.

When I owned Friend Connection we sent detailed questionnaires to several hundred professional men and women ranging in age from their early-twenties to early-fifties. We asked these people about their biggest turn-offs and turn-ons on a date.

I found the results intriguing; seeing ourselves as the other gender sees us can be an eye-opening experience. I've used the survey results to compile the following lists, which are excellent guidelines for anybody who's dating or considering it.

TURN-OFFS: THE BIGGEST MISTAKES MEN AND WOMEN MAKE ON THE FIRST FEW DATES

What women don't like on a date: mistakes men make

1. Not focusing on his date.* Over and over and over, women answering our questionnaires said they disliked it when men did

*You may be interested in knowing that the items with an asterisk also appeared in the men's responses, even though they didn't make the "top seven" list, which follows. Apparently, a significant number of women also make the mistake of not focusing on their dates—talking about an ex too much, talking about *themselves* too much, or being deceitful.

not focus on them. They hated being with a man who looked around the room and noticed every attractive woman who walked in. Of course you're going to notice other attractive women, but do so in a discreet way; don't openly ogle another woman, and above all, *keep yourself focused on your date*. Needless to say, don't flirt with other women, either, not even if the other woman is flirting with you. That is a *big* turn-off for your date.

Being focused also means being sensitive to your date's general comfort and well-being. A woman feels slighted by a man who pays so little attention to her that he doesn't realize if she's cold, if she needs something from the waiter, or if she's clutching the dashboard in mortal terror of his reckless driving. You don't have to be a mind reader to be a considerate date; you just have to pay attention to what's going on.

2. Talking about his ex too much.* It doesn't matter if it's your ex-girlfriend or your ex-wife; it doesn't matter whether your comments are negative or positive. Talking about an ex too much on the first few dates is a big turn-off for your date. Later on, of course, if your relationship progresses to a more intimate level, both of you will naturally share the stories of past relationships that were important to you. But on the first few dates keep the conversation on a lighter note.

3. Talking only about himself,* or being a braggart. No woman wants to be with a man who has an ego so large he can only focus on himself. She doesn't like being with a man who never asks questions about her, who doesn't listen when she talks, and who doesn't ask interesting questions in return. Bragging is even more of a turn-off.

4. Not giving clues about whether or not he is interested in her (or giving false clues). Sometimes you really *don't* know on the first date, and if you don't know, of course it's not right to say, "Let's go out again." But do give some clue about what's going on. If you're pretty sure you'll want to go out with her again, by all means go right ahead and make another date before you say good night. If you're not positive you want to go out with her again and you need some time to reflect on it, at least tell her, "I enjoyed the date." That leaves the possibilities open but doesn't put you on the spot or set her up with false hopes. If you know you're *not* going to ask her out, be courteous. Say, "I really enjoyed the time I spent with you." But do it in a way that you're not leading her to believe you are going to ask her out again.

Dating can give rise to all sorts of self-esteem issues for men and for women. Men often have to deal with rejection simply because they are still most often the ones who are expected to initiate the date. But women all too often experience distress and self-doubt when a man they like promises, "I'll call you," and they never hear from him again.

5. Poor hygiene. You might think that in our odor-conscious culture this wouldn't be a problem, but the women in our surveys indicated differently. If you're going out, use soap and water, and brush your teeth. I don't care if you're dressed impeccably and you look like you stepped out of the pages of *GQ*; if you've got bad breath, you're not going to be very kissable. Be especially conscious of odors if you're a smoker.

6. Patronizing her or talking to her like a child. Some men still do not seem to know how to treat a woman as an intellectual equal. If you talk down to her she will notice it and will most certainly resent it; she may even respond with ego-stinging sarcasm. That's not going to lead to any sort of connection.

7. Lying.* Women hate a man who doesn't tell the truth, and these days, a woman is likely to check you out, whether through digging around on her own or through hiring a private investigator. But even if she doesn't check you out, honesty really is the best policy. A relationship based on lies is no relationship at all.

What men don't like on a date: mistakes women make

1. Lack of appreciation for the man's efforts. This came back over and over on our surveys: a man doesn't like it when his date obviously doesn't appreciate what he's done for her. A man wants you to be happy. If, for example, you indicate that you don't like the restaurant he picked, he will feel personally responsible because he took you there. So do show appreciation for his efforts, even if, given a choice, you would have picked a different restaurant.

2. Complaining a lot, not smiling, and generally not having a good time. In some cases this is symptomatic of the first item—lack of appreciation for the man's efforts—but sometimes the problem goes beyond that. Some women really do seem to be malcontents, complaining over the least little thing: the weather, the traffic, the people across the room who are talking too loudly. Most of these are beyond the man's control anyway; all he can do, and will, if he's wise, is to take her home as quickly as possible.

3. Asking too many personal questions too early on, as if she's quizzing him. There is a difference between asking questions that demonstrate a genuine interest in a person, and interrogating him as if you're going down a checklist for a marital partner. There's plenty of time to find out the more intimate details as the relationship progresses. But if you try to insinuate yourself too soon, you'll scare him away.

As a matter of fact, there were many women in our survey who voiced this complaint against men too. Women don't like to feel that they're being interrogated either. The message here should be obvious: on those first few dates men and women alike would do well to remember two magic words: *Lighten up.*

4. Gold digging. This came out again and again in our surveys. Men want to be loved and appreciated for themselves, and if a man thinks a woman is only interested in whether or not he has money, that's a major turn-off. To avoid any doubts about your motives, don't initiate talk about his financial status this early in the relationship.

5. A woman who is not genuine. Because men seem to be focused so much of the time on a woman's looks, many women make the mistake of underestimating a man's ability to spot a phony personality. As a matter of fact, men are pretty good at detecting pretentiousness in a woman. Ever since you started dating you've probably heard the advice, "Be yourself." That's *always* good advice, particularly when you're on a date.

6. Too much makeup. I suppose you could say this is the aesthetic version of the previous item; at any rate, it came back over and over in our surveys. Men like women who look naturally pretty. They don't care if you wear makeup, as long as it's applied in a way that enhances your natural beauty and doesn't make you look like someone you're not.

Another surprisingly frequent response revealed that men do not like extremely long fingernails painted in vibrant colors. They like well-manicured hands, but they prefer the more natural look.

7. A woman he can't touch. Men don't like a woman who's so obsessed with her looks that she cannot enjoy life—a woman who would be upset if a man touched her hair, or who won't ride in a convertible because she's afraid of getting windblown. This item showed up many times on our surveys.

To summarize:

THE SEVEN BIGGEST MISTAKES MEN MAKE ON THE FIRST FEW DATES

1. NOT FOCUSING ON THEIR DATE
2. TALKING ABOUT THEIR FORMER GIRLFRIENDS OR EX-WIVES TOO MUCH
3. TALKING TOO MUCH ABOUT THEMSELVES, OR BEING A BRAGGART
4. NOT GIVING CLUES ABOUT WHETHER OR NOT THEY ARE INTERESTED IN THE WOMAN (OR GIVING FALSE CLUES)
5. POOR HYGIENE
6. PATRONIZING THE WOMAN OR TREATING HER LIKE A CHILD
7. LYING

THE SEVEN BIGGEST MISTAKES WOMEN MAKE ON THE FIRST FEW DATES

1. LACK OF APPRECIATION FOR THE MAN'S EFFORTS
2. COMPLAINING A LOT, NOT SMILING, NOT HAVING A GOOD TIME
3. ASKING TOO MANY PERSONAL QUESTIONS; QUIZZING THEIR DATE
4. GOLD DIGGING
5. NOT BEING GENUINE
6. WEARING TOO MUCH MAKEUP
7. BEING "UNTOUCHABLE"

That's it for the turn-offs. My intention in giving you these lists of turn-offs is not to make you paranoid or self-conscious, but just to make you aware of potential mistakes. The good news is, *if you're connecting genuinely with people in an honest, open way, using the secrets I've shared, then you won't be making these mistakes anyway.*

TURN-ONS: THE TOP WAYS MEN AND WOMEN CAN IMPRESS THEIR DATES

Now that we've covered the top dating gaffes, let's turn to what women and men *like* on a date. You'll quickly see that many of these items are simply the opposites of those on the "mistakes" lists.

What women like on a date

1. A man who shows genuine interest in her. This seemed to be the number one biggest turn-on for the women in our studies. A woman loves it when she senses that the man she is with is genuinely interested in her. You can demonstrate your interest by actually listening to her and asking questions about what she has to say.

A related item: a woman wants you to let her know where she stands. If you're genuinely interested in seeing her again, let her know. After all, she probably has other pursuers, so you want to make sure you're in the running. If, on the other hand, you're *not* interested in going out with her again, don't lead her on.

2. A man who focuses only on her. One of the best ways you can show you're focused on the woman you're with is to use good eye contact, as we discussed earlier. Don't let your eyes roam all over the room looking at other people; focus in on *her*.

3. A man who behaves like a gentleman. To begin with, most women still like it when you open doors for them. There's been a lot of confusion about this in recent years, but here's a good rule of thumb: Any woman who is openly offended by good manners is probably someone who's so "issue"-oriented that she's not a wonderful prospect for a relationship anyway. It's better to find this out early.

But being a gentleman is more than courtly gestures; it's also a general attitude of consideration for a woman's comfort on a date. It's paying attention to her physical comfort: Is she cold? Does she need something from the waiter? It's also a knack for making a woman feel at ease with you. She needs to feel that if she dropped her fork at the dinner table, or spilled her drink, you wouldn't act as if she'd committed some terrible faux pas.

4. Good hygiene and grooming. You don't have to be the epitome of *GQ* elegance. Just take care of the basics: Shower, comb your hair, brush your teeth, dress in a clean, neat way. And be judicious with your cologne. Even the most expensive designer fragrance can be intolerable if you don't exercise moderation.

5. Physical contact in a tender, caring way. It's not only okay, it's a turn-on if you touch a woman occasionally during the date. Touch her when you're talking to her, or as you're walking to the car together, or walking her to her door. You don't want to touch her in an overtly sexual manner that will make her feel threatened; just touch in a subtle, affectionate way. This will make her feel warmly toward you; it will make her know that you're interested.

6. Flattery, but in a sincere, genuine way. Most women are very good at detecting false flattery. That's why it's so important, in the connecting process, to find something about which you can sincerely compliment a woman. But it's equally important on these first few dates to avoid compliments with sexual overtones. Even if the woman you're with is drop-dead gorgeous, concentrate not on her physical attributes but on her personality and mind.

If she's very attractive, she probably gets many compliments on her looks, anyway. You'll stand out from everybody else if you focus on her inner beauty. Tell her things you really like about her that have nothing to do with her looks; let her know how much you enjoy talking with her, laugh at her jokes. But be sincere. (If you really can't find anything you like about her *but* her looks, I would ask you to consider that perhaps this is not a person with whom you want to have a long-term relationship.)

What men like on a date

1. Good visual appearance. No matter what women might think or how much guys might try to deny it, *men are visual*. There's absolutely no question about it: most men are attracted to you first on a visual basis. So, yes, your appearance is important. But what a man finds physically attractive is not necessarily what our cultural ideals might lead you to think (or fear). Most men are not looking for a men's-magazine centerfold; they simply want a woman who is attractive and who looks the best she can. I'll say the same thing I said to men: take care of the basics. Grooming is important, and so is keeping yourself in shape. This doesn't mean being fashion-model skinny; not only is that an unrealistic goal for most women—and even a health-threatening one—it's not what most men want. Nor do you have to be an aerobics queen or a female bodybuilder. Most men simply like a woman who looks healthy and who exercises.

Hand-in-hand with general physical attractiveness is that winning quality called approachability; men like a woman who looks approachable. What exactly does this mean? It means looking friendly and touchable. A man wants a woman who looks naturally attractive; men don't like a lot of makeup and they definitely like a woman they can touch. They're turned on by a woman if they can touch her hair and it moves. They're delighted by a woman who isn't afraid to get windblown. Here's another tip on looking approachable: Don't wear a lot of jewelry with hearts, and don't wear rings on your left hand. Either of these can give off an ambiguous message, confusing the man as to whether or not you're really available.

2. *A woman with a pleasant, happy voice.* This doesn't mean your voice is sexy and seductive and throaty; it does mean it sounds happy. It means there's a smile in your voice. Men hate to be around women with whiny, complaining voices.

3. *A woman who appreciates his efforts.* Many women don't realize how important it is for a man to feel that he has pleased a woman, that he has won with her. If he brings you flowers and you love them, let him know. If he takes you to a restaurant or club you really like, don't hesitate to express your delight. He's going to feel that it is his responsibility to please you; let him know when he's doing a great job. Even if you're less than completely delighted, show him you appreciate his efforts. Just don't complain, because more than likely he will take any complaint about the date as a personal attack on him.

4. *A woman who is genuinely interested in him.* Men and women are very much alike in this respect. A man wants to know that you're really interested in him; you can show him this throughout the evening by use of eye contact, by focusing in on him and not letting your attention wander, and by really listening to what he has to say and asking him questions. Many men in our surveys said they also like to be touched during the conversation—not sexual or suggestive touching, but just a touch on the shoulder or some other subtle body language that communicates interest.

What about any physical contact beyond that? It is perfectly acceptable to kiss at the end of the first date. It's up to you. If you don't kiss him but you really want him to ask you out again, at least give him a little hug to let him know that you like him. Give him sufficient encouragement to quell that male fear of rejection.

And whether or not you want him to ask you out again, do tell him you had a great time.

5. A woman with confidence. Men like a woman who is confident. This doesn't mean that you're arrogant or domineering; it just means that you're happy within yourself and that you project that happiness outwardly. In turn you'll make *him* feel more confident, and you'll be easy to talk with and be with. In other words, you'll be a good time. That's a real turn-on.

6. A woman who is feminine. Over and over again in our surveys, men said they like a woman who is feminine. I began to question what that meant, and I finally came to the conclusion that it has little to do with being dainty and fragile-looking. Being feminine means you make him recognize his masculinity. In other words, he feels like a man around you. This has nothing to do with old-fashioned, sexist role-playing; I'm talking about the true essence of femininity and masculinity. A man can really own the experience of his masculinity, and really feel like a man, in the presence of a feminine woman.

To summarize:

WOMEN'S SIX BIGGEST TURN-ONS ON A DATE

1. GENUINE INTEREST IN HER
2. FOCUSING ONLY ON HER
3. GENTLEMANLY BEHAVIOR
4. GOOD HYGIENE AND GROOMING
5. PHYSICAL CONTACT IN A TENDER, CARING WAY
6. FLATTERY, BUT IN A SINCERE, GENUINE WAY

MEN'S SIX BIGGEST TURN-ONS ON A DATE

1. GOOD VISUAL APPEARANCE/APPROACHABILITY
2. A PLEASANT, HAPPY VOICE
3. APPRECIATION OF HIS EFFORTS
4. GENUINE INTEREST IN HIM
5. CONFIDENCE
6. FEMININITY

Turn-offs and turn-ons for men and women are not all that different. Whether you're a man or a woman, connecting with someone has to do with being genuine, listening to the other person, being a good time, having fun. Practice these with everyone and you're not going to have any problems on dates.

CRITICAL FLAWS—THE RED FLAGS OF DATING

By now you may be eager to go out and start dating—that's my hope, anyway. But before you go, let's discuss *critical flaws* and how to spot them.

What are critical flaws? They are traits that let you know you do not want to invest your time with this person. If you enter into a relationship with such a person with the hopes of changing that person, you are setting yourself up for years of frustration and grief. How many times have you known of a woman who stayed in an abusive relationship for years, or a man who stuck it out in a relationship with a woman who really didn't love him or didn't want to make a commitment? Don't you deserve better than that?

It's better to be alone, or to just be with your friends, than to invest emotional energy in a relationship with someone who has one or more of the critical flaws listed on the following pages. (And under no circumstance should you ever let yourself become sexually bonded to someone with these flaws. A sexual relationship carries its own set of entanglements, often making a bad relationship more difficult to get out of.)

Many of the critical flaws on this list can be spotted right away, and some are not immediately apparent; but you need to be aware of them all—and you need to know that your wisest course of action, if you do spot one of these flaws, is to end the relationship.

Critical flaws to watch out for:

1. *Addictions of any kind.* If a person is addicted to something—anything—you will *never* be a priority in that person's life. Addiction can be to a substance—alcohol or other drugs, or to a behavior—gambling, spending money, even obsessive exercising. Some purists insist that "addiction" is a misnomer when applied to a behavior, but I'm not going to get into an argument over semantics. A person displaying any sort of addictive behavior is most likely poor relationship material.

If you keep your eyes open you can usually see signs, on the first few dates, that the person has addictive tendencies. Sometimes it's obvious, as when a person drinks excessively (unless it happens to be New Year's Eve, or the two of you are at Mardi Gras or Carnivál in Rio. Under ordinary circumstances, however, a person who has a need to get extremely drunk on the first date may have a very serious problem). Or you might pick up conversational cues; perhaps the person talks in a manner that indicates an addictive or obsessive nature. If you're not sure about the signs of addiction, there are plenty of books that go into detail on this subject. If *anything* about this person suggests an addictive tendency of any sort, steer clear.

It is not your job to "save" or change another person. You cannot do it. Please do not go for potential, for what you think that person could be "if only" the addiction problem could be solved. Get out immediately, and find someone who is adequate as is.

2. *A person who has a lot of anger or rage.* If a person has a real problem with anger or rage, it's going to come out sooner or later. If you're observant, you'll be able to detect clues early on. Often you can tell by the person's conversation or behavior—for example, if the person expresses inappropriate hostility toward an ex-spouse, or explodes into rage at a waiter for a trivial reason, or displays unusually aggressive behind-the-wheel behavior. If you have any doubts at all, don't stick around and risk having that rage vented on you. Know that you are not safe with a person who has a rage problem; the newspapers are filled with stories of people who paid for this knowledge with their lives. Get out now.

3. A person who's controlling or overbearing. Very often, this goes along with uncontrollable rage. But even if rage or anger is not a problem, a person who is very controlling, or who has an overbearing nature, is not somebody you want to be with. These people are insufferable; they want to control every little thing. More than likely they'll want to control you, too. You do *not* want to be in a relationship with a person who dominates you and doesn't give you freedom to grow.

4. A person who has a chronic noncommitment problem. Unless he or she is very, very young, somebody with no history of long-term relationships is probably a poor relationship risk. The person doesn't necessarily have to have been married; these days many people wait till their thirties or even their forties to get married for the first time. But if the person has not had even one long-term relationship, what does that tell you about his or her willingness or capability to make a commitment? Be very cautious here.

5. A person who's emotionally unavailable. Perhaps the person is married, or not over a former relationship, or permanently hung up on someone else, or perhaps just "married" to his or her work. *In any case, this person is not going to be there for you.*

The married person, for example, is probably *not* going to leave his or her spouse, despite earnest or tearful promises to the contrary. My friend Rita adds a bit of hard-earned wisdom to this caveat: "Even if they do leave the spouse, you'll probably end up being the 'transitional' relationship. More than likely you'll soon be left out in the cold, as I was when my married lover left his wife. I thought he was leaving her for me—we'd even found an apartment we were going to move into together—but then, the next thing I heard, he'd run off to Florida with a brand-new girlfriend. Admittedly my story is a bit unusual; it's much more common for a guy to just go back home to his wife. In either case, *you* come out the loser. My advice is, NEVER date anybody who is married."

Married or not, a person who for *any* reason is emotionally unavailable will make you feel forever like an outsider, pounding on the door to be let in.

6. A person who is a chronic victim. Granted, our culture seems to encourage "victimism" in many ways. But that doesn't make the chronic victim any more pleasant to be around, and this is certainly not the kind of person you want to have a relationship with. You can easily recognize the signs of people with victim-consciousness; they're always talking about all the bad things that have happened to them. And none of these bad things are ever their fault. It's the government, or a terrible ex-spouse, or the parents who just never understood, or anyone but the "victims" themselves. You don't want a relationship with someone who is unable to take responsibility for his or her own life.

7. A person who constantly dwells on personal issues or past mistakes. If our culture encourages victimism, it also seems to encourage people to focus, to the point of obsession, on their personal "issues"—their childhood traumas, their phobias, their recovery (from addictions, painful relationships, or whatever). A healthy focus on personal growth is wonderful; I'm all for it. And I think the recovery movement and twelve-step programs have done wonders for countless people. But there has to be a balance, and there are some people who are so caught up in their own dramas that they're not really growing. They're also pretty tiresome to be around. You don't want to be part of those endless dramas, do you?

Then there are those people who continually dwell on their past mistakes. Listen closely to such a person and you'll probably detect a pattern of repeating the same mistakes over and over. What does that tell you? It tells you that the person is not learning from his or her mistakes. It also gives you a pretty good idea of what your future with this person would be. You don't want to be just another "mistake" in somebody's life. Get out now, and find a partner who's willing to grow and have a real relationship.

8. A narcissistic or self-centered person. A relationship is all about give and take. Unfortunately, a person who's completely self-centered or narcissistic cannot give. Ironically, the narcissistic person is incapable of self-love, and is therefore not capable of loving anyone else, either. There are all kinds of signs to watch out for. To begin with, if the person's only topic of conversation is "me, me, me," that's a pretty good sign of self-centeredness right there. Also see item 7. You don't want a person who is incapable of focusing on other people.

9. A person who's immature or chronically irresponsible. This shows up in many ways. Look for signs that the person is irresponsible financially or in other ways, or is neglectful of self or dependents, pets, or property. For example, let's say you're a woman whose date is being very cagey about his living arrangements. Your first suspicion may be that he's married and doesn't want you to know, but that might not be the problem at all. It could be that he's simply too embarrassed to let you know he's been living rent-free in his parents' basement for the past five years because he can't hold down a job. Or let's say you're a man, and your date invites you over to her apartment, but you see signs of gross neglect such as plants or pets in desperate need of attention, or a kitchen sink piled up with six months' worth of dirty dishes. Or maybe you're a woman who's just found out that the guy you're dating owes his ex-wife two years of back child-support payments, while he's been living an affluent lifestyle and spending money like there's no tomorrow. If you see any signs of irresponsibility such as this, get out. You don't have a whole person to deal with in the beginning; there's no chance of a successful relationship.

10. A person who is promiscuous. You simply don't need this. Even if it weren't for the deadly threat of AIDS, from an emotional standpoint a promiscuous person is a very poor risk for a relationship. If you are looking for a serious monogamous relationship and you see signs of promiscuity in that person, just get out. And there are plenty of signs. Blatant flirtation with people besides you is not only one of the biggest turn-offs on a date, it could be a real indicator of a wandering libido. The person who has a problem with being faithful is not likely to change.

AVOID A PERSON WITH CRITICAL FLAWS SUCH AS . . .

1. ADDICTIONS
2. ANGER OR RAGE
3. A CONTROLLING OR OVERBEARING PERSONALITY
4. A CHRONIC NONCOMMITMENT PROBLEM
5. EMOTIONAL UNAVAILABILITY
6. VICTIM CONSCIOUSNESS
7. OBSESSION WITH PERSONAL ISSUES OR PAST MISTAKES
8. NARCISSISM OR SELF-CENTEREDNESS
9. IMMATURITY OR CHRONIC IRRESPONSIBILITY
10. PROMISCUITY

AND THEN THERE ARE THE DEADLY TIME BOMBS . . .

You should also look for factors that might not be a problem now, but could be a problem in the future. Think back to the list you made in chapter one, where you wrote down the attributes of your perfect person. You may have decided some of the items were negotiable, such as age, spiritual orientation, etc. But these issues, or any others on the following list, should merit your most careful consideration.

1. ***Religious or spiritual differences.*** If you're a very spiritual person and strongly believe in God, and the other person doesn't, that could become a problem. Or if the two of you are of different faiths, it could become a problem if children enter

into the picture; in what faith will you raise the children? Think about this carefully.

2. ***Big age differences can definitely be a problem***. Right now it might not be an issue, but if the age gap is more than, say, ten years, consider what the relationship will be like even a few years from now. Think of what it will be like in ten or twenty years. If there is a significant age difference, you may want to reconsider.
3. ***A hostile ex-spouse who's still involved in the person's life.*** Knowing there is an ex-spouse is one thing; putting up with angry or threatening phone calls at three o'clock in the morning is quite another. Be very aware of the problems you might be getting into.
4. ***Children that you've met and know that you could never get along with.*** There are books, magazine articles, and TV shows about the challenges of the blended family. Are you up to these challenges? Even if the person's children are not going to be living with you, even if they live in another state, if there's any animosity at all it is going to be a problem sooner or later. You have to decide if this person is worth it. If you cannot accept the children, or vice versa, the relationship is going to have real problems.
5. ***Different social or ethnic backgrounds.*** It's not that biracial relationships, or relationships between people of radically different social backgrounds, cannot work. Many of them work very well. But if one or both of you lack the strength and maturity to deal with societal and family pressures (which can be considerable), the relationship does not have a very good chance of succeeding.
6. ***Long-distance relationships.*** She lives and works in California, he lives and works in London. They're deeply in love and committed to each other. While this may seem terribly romantic, there are many pitfalls to long-distance relationships. Exorbitant long-distance phone bills are just the beginning. The strain of never, or rarely, seeing each other can really take its toll on a relationship; absence does not necessarily make the heart grow fonder. Another common problem, if the rela-

> tionship does last, is that it remains forever suspended in the "infatuation" stage. It never really becomes a real relationship. More often than not, "long-term" and "long-distance" do *not* go together.

Please carefully consider these critical flaws and deadly time bombs. Don't just let things happen; make a choice with your life. If you think the relationship is not going to work out for you because of one or more of the reasons just given, then make a clear choice not to extend it. Choose not to continue to get attached and bonded to that person.

THE BIG BAD C'S: DON'T DO THESE!

I know I've been giving you lots of lists in this chapter; well, here's yet another one. Let's call it the list of the "bad C's." You want to watch yourself when you're on a date, and make sure you don't do these things; after all, you don't want the other person to think *you* have critical flaws. These are seven C's you *don't* want to sail:

DON'T . . .

1. CLING
2. COMPLAIN
3. CRITICIZE
4. CONDEMN
5. HAVE CONTEMPT
6. CONTROL
7. COMPETE

When it comes right down to it, all of these points are just common sense. All you have to do is learn to pay attention to your behavior. That way you can catch yourself when you slip, replacing "bad" conduct with behavior that is consistent with your desire to connect with another person.

A FEW MORE POINTS ABOUT THOSE FIRST FEW DATES

No matter how well-versed you are in dating theory, what really counts is practice. And, particularly if you're a bit out of practice, you might be facing that first date with a bit of apprehension. I hope you know by now that dating, even the first date with someone you barely know, does not have to be a painful process. It all depends on where you place your focus; it is my hope that you'll be focusing *not* on yourself and the impression you're making—but on the fact that you're connecting, opening up, and really listening to the other person.

I am positive you'll find that if you're concentrating on the other person instead of on how you think you're being perceived, you will sail through the first date and be well on your way to a second one (if that's what you want).

WHAT IF YOU WANT TO GO OUT AGAIN, BUT THE OTHER PERSON DOESN'T?

FOR WOMEN: ***What happens if a man doesn't call back after that first date?*** This means you have a decision to make. There are all kinds of reasons a man doesn't call back. It may *not* be that he's not interested. First of all, don't expect him to call back too soon. Even if the two of you got along splendidly on your date, sometimes a man really just has to think about whether or not he wants to ask you out again. It may be a week before you hear from him. At any rate, I'd suggest you give him at least a week; if you haven't heard from him within that time, it doesn't hurt for you to call. Keep the conversation on a casual level: "We were talking about tai chi; I noticed there's a new book out about it and I wanted to let you know." If the problem was that the man thought *you* weren't interested, this will show him you are. If he's the one who's not interested, this will give you a chance to pick up clues about that. If you can't really pick up any clues but he doesn't follow up after that, I'd advise you to go look for someone else. Move on; don't use all of your energy on someone who isn't interested.

FOR MEN: ***What happens if you call the woman back after the first date, and she doesn't return your call?*** If you call the woman back and she doesn't return your call, call one more time. There's always the possibility that her roommate forgot to give her the message. But I'll say the same thing to you that I said to women: if it turns out that she's absolutely not interested, move on. Don't ever put too much energy into someone who's not interested in you. You want a reciprocal relationship where your needs are getting met.

Whether you're a man or a woman, you simply don't want to put time and energy into any relationship that isn't meeting your needs.

NEVER PURSUE SOMEONE WHO IS OBVIOUSLY NOT INTERESTED IN YOU

But let's say everybody has called everyone back as expected, and things are going along well, and a second date is in the offing. By the second date, you're getting to know each other a little better. Again, your concentration should be on having fun. You'll be learning more about the other person, but that should come in the natural flow of things. Don't force it, don't dig, don't ask prying questions. Intimacy is a process that develops; you cannot have instant intimacy.

By the third date, you'll probably both be making decisions about how much you want to invest in this relationship. Also, by the second and third dates, you should be able to detect the signs of any critical flaws in this person.

Even though there's so much going on with these first dates, don't forget your focus should be on having fun. Go to a funny movie or a comedy club, and laugh together. Go bowling or waterskiing or in-line skating. Engage in some sort of activity where you're laughing, sharing energy and ideas, and having a good time. What's important is that you're going through the stages of connecting.

THE HAZARDS (BESIDES THE OBVIOUS) OF HAVING SEX TOO SOON

The average date on which people have sex is the third date. I absolutely do not recommend having sex so early in a relationship. We're going to talk about this subject much more in the next chapter, but I do want to say now that sex is too important a decision to be taken lightly. Of course it has always been important from an emotional standpoint, but these days it's a life-threatening issue as well. These first few dates are all about connecting; *entering into a sexual relationship too soon can abort the connection process.* I strongly recommend you save the sex for later.

AFTER THE DATE: QUESTIONNAIRES FOR THE OVERLY ANALYTICAL AND THE OVERLY EMOTIONAL

Now I'm going to give you a tool to help you decide if the person you're going out with is someone you'll want to be spending more time with. You could just stumble through these early stages of the relationship and let whatever happens happen. That's what most people do. More than likely it's what you've always done. But that hasn't worked very well in the past, has it? I didn't think so. Let's try something different, then. I'm going to give you a set of questionnaires to review *after* your first date, your second date, and your third date with a person. The purpose of these questionnaires is to provide you with a chance to really reflect on your feelings, in order to determine if there is real potential for a continuing relationship with this person.

You'll notice that there are two sections to each questionnaire. That's because they were designed to address two different types of people: those who are too analytical, and those who are too emotional. You probably already know which category you fall into, but I'm going to elaborate a bit because I want to make a point about the need for balance.

We'll talk about you analytical types first. You're the

"thinkers"—the people who tend to intellectualize, even in dating situations. Rather than ask yourself questions such as, "How did I feel? Did I have fun? Was it a good time?" you methodically go through your mental (or written) checklists and ask questions that you think will help you determine: "Is this the right person for me?" This tendency to intellectualize is typical of engineers and other people who are very logical and cerebral.

I have nothing but admiration for people with sharp minds, but sometimes it's possible to be too analytical, and that can cause you to miss out on a chance at true happiness. A man I'll call Roger is a case in point. Roger had some very set notions about the type of woman he desired for a life mate. One of his requirements was a woman who was highly educated, preferably with a graduate degree or two. Roger himself has multiple degrees, and he felt that only a similarly credentialed woman would be able to "keep up with him."

When he met Sheila there was an immediate mutual attraction. They came from similar backgrounds, were the same age, had the same taste in music and food, they shared many interests, and they had great chemistry. There was no denying that Sheila was intelligent and witty; they had fascinating conversations on those first few dates. But Sheila didn't have a college degree. She had dropped out of school to go to work when she was a few credits short of the requirements for a B.A., and she had never gone back. Even though she had a lively spirit, a curious mind, and an obvious hunger for new knowledge and experiences, she didn't have the credentials Roger considered essential in a life mate. Although he had the tact not to admit this to Sheila, to him her lack of a degree indicated a lack of persistence and discipline. Somewhat reluctantly he decided not to see her anymore.

Eventually Sheila ended up marrying somebody else, but Roger still thinks about her with regret. He now knows that he should have paid more attention to his emotions, to the way he felt when he was with this woman, and to the way she felt about him, than to criteria that were, after all, pretty superficial. He says, "The next time I meet someone like Sheila—if I'm lucky enough to meet someone like her—I'm going to be more aware of what I'm feeling instead of how she measures up to some arbitrary list of credentials."

On the flip side of the coin, some of us are too emotional. We're the "feelers." If you're this type, you may end up going out with somebody who is all wrong for you. I have a friend I'll call Marianne, who is a feeler. She met an attractive man at a music festival, and he turned out to be a member of a motorcycle gang. But even after she found that out, it didn't faze her; he was handsome and, in fact, his "bad-boy" image was a little exciting. She got all caught up in connecting with him, being interested in him, listening to his stories of adventures on the road.

The truth is, she got carried away with the excitement. She was not using her logical side because, if she had, she would have said right away, "Hey, this might not be the best match for me. Maybe this isn't a relationship I should pursue."

She went out on a couple of dates with him, but quickly came back down to earth on the second date, when he casually mentioned having served prison time for assault and battery. It was then that Marianne said to herself, "I don't know, maybe this isn't such a good deal and, you know, motorcycles can be dangerous." Marianne's story has a happy ending: she stopped seeing the man, and he moved on down the road, but she did worry her friends and family along the way. If she had tapped into her logical side at the beginning, she could have avoided the problem altogether.

The intellect and the emotions are equally necessary and important. Deny either, and you can end up making some costly mistakes. It's true that some people are naturally more analytical and some are naturally more emotional. I'm certainly not suggesting you try to change your basic nature. But you do need to have balance. That's why I'm giving you these "two-sided" questionnaires. Answer the questions in both sections of each questionnaire, but really spend some time with the section that addresses the personality type that's the *opposite* of yours, for this is where you'll gain the most insight.

Even if you're not currently dating, do look over the following questions so you'll have an idea what they are. And be sure to come back and answer them when you have begun dating. Set up the appropriate number of pages in your Relationship Journal. Be sure to repeat this question-and-answer process for each person you go out with.

The First Date

Emotional Questions for Analytical People

1. Did we both have fun?
2. Were we both comfortable?
3. Was there laughter?
4. Did we touch in a tender way?
5. Were we able to focus on and connect with each other?
6. Were we attracted to each other intellectually, emotionally, physically?
7. Were we complimentary to each other?
8. Did we truly listen to each other?
9. Were we open and honest with each other?
10. Did we treat each other respectfully?

Analytical Questions for Emotional People

1. Are we the right age range for each other?
2. Do we each have the physical qualities the other one is looking for?
3. Are we of the same education level?
4. Has he/she been married before?
5. Does he/she have children already?
6. Do we have similar goals?
7. Was there good communication?
8. Does he/she have personal habits (such as smoking or drinking) that are not compatible with mine?
9. Do we have similar lifestyles?
10. Are we geographically compatible?

THE SECOND DATE

NOTE: AFTER YOUR SECOND DATE, REVIEW YOUR RESPONSES FROM THE FIRST DATE AND THEN ANSWER THESE QUESTIONS.

Emotional Questions for Analytical People

1. ARE WE GENUINELY INTERESTED IN EACH OTHER?
2. WERE WE BOTH COMFORTABLE THIS TIME?
3. WERE WE BECOMING MORE ATTRACTED TO EACH OTHER INTELLECTUALLY, EMOTIONALLY, PHYSICALLY?
4. WAS THE CHEMISTRY STILL THERE?
5. WERE WE AT EASE SHARING REAL FEELINGS WITH EACH OTHER?

Analytical Questions for Emotional People

1. IS THIS PERSON SHOWING ANY CRITICAL FLAWS? (SEE THE SECTION EARLIER IN THIS CHAPTER, ON CRITICAL FLAWS.)
2. HAS HE/SHE HAD SUCCESSFUL RELATIONSHIPS IN THE PAST?
3. IS HE/SHE LOOKING FOR THE SAME TYPE OF RELATIONSHIP THAT I'M LOOKING FOR?
4. IS HIS/HER BELIEF SYSTEM SIMILAR TO MINE?
5. DOES HE/SHE HAVE A POSITIVE ATTITUDE TOWARD LIFE?

THE THIRD DATE

BY THE THIRD DATE, YOU SHOULD BE FEELING MORE COMFORTABLE WITH THE PERSON, AND YOU ARE PROBABLY MOVING TOWARD A PHYSICAL RELATIONSHIP. REVIEW AND EVALUATE YOUR RESPONSES FROM THE FIRST TWO DATES BEFORE ANSWERING THESE QUESTIONS.

Emotional Questions for Analytical People

1. DO WE FEEL SAFE WITH EACH OTHER?
2. DO WE DISPLAY AFFECTION TOWARD EACH OTHER IN A TENDER, LOVING MANNER?

3. Do we honor and respect each other's feelings?
4. Do we feel romantic toward each other?
5. Do we genuinely like each other?

Analytical Questions for Emotional People

1. Do we fill each other's basic needs? (Refer to the lists in chapter two.)
2. Have we discussed STDs (sexually transmitted diseases) and protection? (This subject is discussed further in chapter four.)
3. Would we be good companions for each other?
4. Would we be good sexual partners for each other?
5. Could we be good friends to each other?

Review your responses to all of these questions after the first three dates, and evaluate whether or not you should continue dating this person. If you feel you need more time to get real answers to some of the questions, continue to date the person. However, if you feel there are critical flaws in the person, or that you cannot meet each other's needs (as listed in chapter two), I suggest you move on and continue meeting new and more compatible people.

Be sure, however, that you weigh both the emotional and the analytical responses before making any decisions.

♥ ♥ ♥

Connecting with people is one of the most important skills you'll ever learn; it helps you in all areas of your life, whether business or personal. If you practice what you've learned in this chapter you'll find yourself becoming better and better at connecting. You'll discover you're making more solid connections with more positive people—and that, my friend, will enable you to have a better life.

♥ The Fourth Principle ♥

CHEMISTRY

Chemistry is the elusive quality that separates a romantic relationship from a platonic one. It's the special attraction, the magical essence that makes us want to have sex with a particular person, to blend and be one with that person. Because chemistry is such a powerful force, however, it has to be handled carefully.

If you've done the exercises outlined in the first three chapters, you've begun to learn how to connect with other people, to be more open, to smile, and to be more confident. In short, you're learning to genuinely link with the people around you. And now, perhaps, you've established a special link with one person in particular; having taken care of all the prerequisites and established intellectual and emotional intimacy, you are considering taking the relationship to the next step: physical intimacy.

In other words, chemistry has entered the picture. Perhaps it was there all along, but you've reached the point where you can no longer ignore it.

Before we go any further, however, I want to take a moment to address the concerns of those who might take issue with my placing the chapter on sex at this point in the book instead of closer to the end, perhaps in conjunction with the chapter on commitment. I have, after all, given much emphasis to studying these principles in order, and I am sensitive to the fact that some people still believe sex should not be a consideration at all until two people have decided to make a commitment—which, to traditionalists, means marriage.

While I respect everybody's beliefs, I also feel it is my responsibility to offer advice that reflects contemporary reality rather than traditional ideals. And, speaking from the perspective of one who has spent over a decade working with thousands of contemporary men and women, I have to say that most couples in our society *do* have sex before they are married—and, in many cases, before the issue of marriage or any other sort of commitment even comes up. That's why I felt it was important to place the chemistry chapter at this point in the book. How you handle the sequence of events in your own relationship is, of course, up to you and your partner. If your choice is to be celibate until marriage, more power to you. *In any case, this chapter contains information that I believe is valid no matter when you and your partner choose to begin your sexual relationship.*

There's no denying that chemistry stirs things up; when it is working, it sometimes makes us behave in a manner completely atypical of our normal patterns. It can make us a little crazy. Everyone reacts differently when attracted to someone. Some people get that starry look in their eyes and become very suave and debonair. Other people act like Goofy and sound like Minnie Mouse. They become uncoordinated, clumsy, and appear to be more socially retarded than they actually are.

The exquisite tension between the hunger we feel for that special person, and the actual fulfillment of that hunger, can cause dramatic changes in the way we behave.

So let's examine this chemistry business. How important is it? How do we know it's there? How do we deal with it? How can we make sex magical, and how can we make the magic last?

THE STAGES OF ATTRACTION—THE TIMETABLE DIFFERS FOR EVERYBODY

Let me address a few basic questions first. Several people have asked me whether a relationship, even a marriage, can last if the chemistry simply isn't there. My response is to ask the person, "How important is sex to you?"

If sex is very important to you, a relationship is not going to last without that chemistry. You can't make it up. You can't create it. It's either there or it isn't. You should realize, however, that this element which we clumsily refer to as chemistry doesn't necessarily arrive at the same time for all people.

People have also asked me, "Well, how do you know when the chemistry is there?" This may seem like a silly question to anybody who has ever been hit hard by Cupid's arrow. It may be pretty tempting to say, "Hey, when it's there, you *know*." But that doesn't really answer the question, does it? And it is, after all, a legitimate question.

I think it's helpful to understand the different types of attraction. People experience attraction on three basic levels:

1. ***Intellectual.*** When you become attracted to someone on an intellectual level, you start to share and exchange ideas with each other. You are mentally intrigued and challenged by the other person.
2. ***Emotional.*** You feel safe enough with this person to share your most intimate thoughts. You can talk about your past, your future dreams, and even your deepest fears, knowing your trust will not be betrayed in any way. You long to explore the depth of that safety, to know that this person is truly a "safe harbor" for *all* your feelings.
3. ***Physical.*** Now, *this* is chemistry, and when it hits, everything changes. You think this has to be the most appealing person in the whole universe. The woman looks at her man's hands and thinks, "These must be the most beautiful hands in all of creation. Michelangelo would have loved to immortalize the exquisite lines of this man's hands"—and she is absolutely focused on her desire to feel the touch of those hands on her body. The man looks at her and thinks, "She has the softest skin of any woman in the world," and nothing consumes him so completely as his desire to simply brush his fingertips across its smoothness. He looks at her mouth and all he can think about is kissing her. I'm censoring this somewhat, of course, but you get my drift. At any rate, *this is chemistry!* The poet Richard Brautigan once wrote a brief, yet clear poem paying homage to chemistry. It reads, "Forget about Love! I want to die in your yellow hair." This is the kind of chemistry that makes you heat up, wanting nothing more than to blend together, to be one—in other words, to have sex with that person, again and again.

There is a fourth level of attraction, one which generally occurs after the other levels have been fairly well established. This is connection on a spiritual level. Of course this is not the place to go into this topic in detail; that's worthy of a whole book in itself. When the spiritual connection is there, you both know it.

The point to all this is that, ideally, you should feel attraction on all of the first three levels—intellectual, emotional, and chemical—before you ever begin a sexual relationship. But people are individuals, not ideals, and sometimes relationships get off to a bumpy start because *not all people go through this process in the same orderly fashion*. Some people are attracted first by chemistry. Other people are attracted first intellectually. This may result in a relationship which begins with one person "in lust" while the other is merely "intrigued." This lack of symmetry may lead both people to give up too early because "it just isn't going to work." What they need to do is to take some more time with each other, to see if their levels of attraction begin to synchronize.

Let me give you some examples. I've heard a number of men state that they can generally tell within five minutes of meeting a woman whether or not a relationship potential exists. This is because men are, for the most part, prone to respond first on the level of physical attractiveness. That isn't to say that some women don't respond on that same level, but it's more prevalent in men.

Jack is a case in point. A couple of years ago Jack's cousin fixed him up with a blind date. Quite unlike the blind dates of everybody's worst nightmare, Barbara turned out to be drop-dead gorgeous. She looked, in fact, like the woman of Jack's dreams. "She bore a striking resemblance to a cheerleader I'd dated in college," he told me, "five-feet-six, 120 pounds, great body, perfect skin, long blond hair, with a smile that took my breath away. I was speechless. I was in love." I don't know about love at that early stage, but Jack most certainly had been thunderstruck by chemistry.

Barbara's perspective is slightly different. "I answered the door that first night, and I thought to myself, *Hmm, he's a very good-looking man. That's nice*. But to tell the truth, I wasn't overwhelmed. I guess I was registering his good looks as a fact to file away. Anyway, we had a great time that night; he was funny and interesting and I knew I definitely wanted to see him again. Well, the more we went out, the more I liked him . . . and, as they say, the rest is history."

Indeed, Jack and Barbara just got married. It's pretty obvious that Barbara did not find Jack unattractive; it's just that she is a person who tends to respond first on an intellectual level.

What happens if you're the person who is initially attracted on an intellectual level, and you're going out with someone who is attracted first on a physical level? Some definite problems can arise.

Dorothy, a forty-two-year-old professional chef, can speak to this issue very well. "I'm a person who is never attracted on a physical level first—well, at least it's never happened to me so far," she tells me. "I almost always hook up first on an intellectual level. I might see a man and *think* he's very attractive, yet not *feel* particularly attracted to him. For me, the sequence generally goes like this: first, I'm intellectually attracted to someone; second, I'm emotionally attracted to him; and then, third, that feeling of physical attraction hits me—seemingly from out of nowhere. Usually it hits me so suddenly, it amazes me. But it never happens right away. I have to develop a relationship with the person first."

Dorothy recently met a man at a friend's party. She liked him well enough, and it was obvious to her that he was very physically attracted to her. They began going out. However, even though she felt there was a chance she might eventually be equally enamored, she needed more time to sort through her feelings. But he didn't want to wait. So what happened?

"I'll tell you what *didn't* happen," she answers. "A relationship never had the chance to develop. There seemed to be real potential, and who knows, he might have even been the man of my dreams, but we'll never know, because he didn't give me a chance. He was just too intense at the beginning, and he scared me off."

WHEN CHEMISTRY HITS, PROCEED WITH CAUTION

Olivia, a computer programmer who's a long-time member of the video dating service I used to own, tells me of an experience she had a while back. "I was casually seeing a man to whom I was intellectually attracted," she says. "We spent time exchanging great business ideas and a lot of creative ideas in general. He was a very intelligent man and I really liked him but, at that point, I didn't feel any measurable physical attraction toward him. However, even though he never made any overt moves, I sensed he was physically attracted to me.

"Once in a while I get very bad migraine headaches, and I happened to be having one on a night I was out with this man. Some time ago I discovered that having my feet rubbed helps ease the migraine. So my date offered to rub my feet, and as he was doing this—WHAM—that chemistry came from out of nowhere and hit me full force. All of a sudden I felt *very* physically attracted to him.

"The problem was, I still didn't feel emotionally safe with him. While I certainly felt intellectually attracted, I didn't know enough about him to truly feel emotionally safe. My immediate reaction was to retreat, and fast. It took me a long time, after that, to decide whether I wanted a relationship with that person, because I had to pull so far away from him early on. I had to back away so that I didn't get confused. I did not want to let myself be blinded by lust to the point where I could not see what he was really about."

Fortunately Olivia's friend did not try to push the issue. He respected her need for time to evaluate the situation. As time went on and Olivia got to know this man better, she found more and more traits that led her to conclude that he would not be a suitable partner for her. "Nothing horrible," she explains, "just the fact that, basically, he's more emotionally distant than I'd want my life mate to be. As an acquaintance and business associate he's terrific, he's a lot of fun, but I would never be happy in a relationship with him.

"I'm so glad I pulled back," she concludes. "I really think that if I'd acted on that first spark of physical attraction before I felt truly safe, it would have been a big mistake. Almost certainly I would have ruined a fine friendship."

I would suggest that you take a cue from Dorothy and Olivia and exercise similar caution when chemistry enters the picture.

THE TWO BIG REASONS NOT TO JUMP THE GUN

We've established that, ideally, we should know a person fairly well before we have sex. We all know equally well, however, how effectively our logic is dismissed when confronted with sexual desire. When we really *want* someone, all our high-minded ideologies turn into flies, buzzing around and distracting us from what we're focused on. Before you go swatting those little flies away, you might want to consider the consequences. When you let yourself get confused or blinded by lust, there's a very good chance you will enter into a sexual relationship with ***(1) the wrong person,*** or ***(2) the right person at the wrong time.*** Either one of these scenarios can have serious consequences for your happiness.

The ties that bind are not always blessed

Let's talk about that first possibility: Having sex with a person who's totally wrong for you. Once you establish a sexual bond with a person, you've established a link that is often there for keeps. For better or worse, sex completely changes the dynamics of a relationship.

Some people say sex is the glue that keeps relationships together. It can just as easily be the glue that keeps a relationship together long after you have decided you want it to end. When you're overcome with physical attraction it's very easy to be totally blinded to a person's imperfections, even to any critical flaws that person may have.

Miranda first met Dennis at a popular nightspot. He was stunningly good-looking and had a wicked sense of humor. Though he had an almost overbearing personality, he was, all in all, the sexiest man she had ever met. The sexual energy between Miranda and Dennis was absolutely compelling; they went to his apartment and made love that same night. Dennis was a bit rough and demanding, but for Miranda, that just added to his mystique.

They began going out on a regular basis, even though several of Miranda's friends warned her about his reputation for being temperamental and abusive. Somebody even told her that there were rumors that he had hit his ex-wife a few times. She discounted these warnings, reasoning that her friends were envious. It was true that Dennis would occasionally put her down in front of others, usually when he'd had a bit too much to drink, but he wasn't exactly what she would call verbally abusive. Besides, Miranda rationalized that his taunting her was just a manifestation of his sarcastic sense of humor. On a few occasions he brought her to tears, but he would always apologize to her profusely the next day.

Against the advice of her friends and family, Miranda married Dennis a few months after they met. She soon began to have second thoughts about her choice. To begin with, Dennis became very jealous and possessive of her, to the point where he would interrogate her when she came home from a shopping trip with her female friends. Soon she couldn't walk out the door without getting the third degree. At the same time, Dennis himself had no qualms about straying. She lived in terror that he would give her AIDS or some other sexually transmitted disease.

To make matters worse, Dennis grew progressively more abusive verbally. He'd still apologize when he made her cry, but a day or so later he was back to his old tricks. They began fighting more and more frequently, mostly over trivial matters, and the fight was almost always initiated by Dennis.

The first time Dennis hit her, he gave her a black eye. It was then that Miranda told him she was going to leave him. But he apologized so sincerely, even agreeing to go to counseling, that she decided to give him a second chance. After all, she still loved him, and besides, once in a while the sex was still fantastic.

A year later, Miranda was giving Dennis his hundredth "second chance." In the intervening time she'd suffered several black eyes, various bumps and bruises, and even a broken rib from his abuse. She had been hospitalized twice. Finally she really did leave him, but he stalked her for two weeks, alternately threatening her and showering her with gifts and flowers, promising her that this time he really would make an effort to change. The night she came home to him, they made love more passionately than they ever had. For a few days he was a model of good behavior. But before a week was up, Miranda had another black eye.

Unlike most of these situations, Miranda's tale has a happy ending. She finally left Dennis again and went to stay with a friend who lives in another state. She has initiated divorce proceedings—apparently a wake-up call for Dennis, because he finally has entered counseling. Though she says she has no desire to go back to him, Miranda wishes Dennis well and is proud of him for taking what was, in fact, a very courageous step.

"Leaving Dennis was the hardest thing I ever did," Miranda says. "It was even more difficult because at the time I left I thought I might be pregnant." (Fortunately she wasn't.) She adds that she wishes she hadn't been so quick to get sexually involved with him. "If I'd just waited a little longer, and gotten to know him a little better," she says, "I would have seen the warning signs that everybody else saw from the beginning. I could have saved myself a lifetime of grief."

Granted, Miranda's case is extreme, but the lesson is well taken whether or not physical abuse is an issue. *Becoming sexually bonded with someone who is, for any reason, bad for you is one of the worst mistakes you can make.* Because that bond, once established, can be very difficult to break—and because things get even more complicated if children result from the bond—it's always best not to have sex with someone until you are really sure about the person. A lifetime of misery is too high a price to pay for a few nights of passion.

Buck naked and scared silly?!?

If sex can be the glue that keeps even a bad relationship alive, it can also, ironically, be the death of a good relationship, if the timing isn't right. For years movies and novels have given us variations of the "instant-fireworks" scenario, wherein two virtual strangers fall into bed together, have perfect sex, fall in love, and live happily ever after. There's no denying this makes a good story, but, having heard hundreds of stories from *real* couples, I can give you a much more likely scenario:

Imagine that you're with someone who's really pretty wonderful. There are no red flags popping up in your head, no signs that this person has critical flaws, no indication that sex with this individual would be a ghastly mistake. Quite the contrary—you've been out together a couple of times, things are going well between you, and the chemistry has hit full force. Everything seems quite natural. Maybe this truly is the perfect person for you.

So here you are, in bed together for the first time.

And suddenly you realize *you are buck naked, staring straight into the eyes of somebody who is, for all practical purposes, a stranger.* There you are, absolutely exposed to someone you really don't know at all, on the verge of participating in the most intimate act two human beings can possibly do together. So how do you feel? Romantic? Overwhelmed with passion?

No, more than likely *you're scared silly*—or, at the very least, you're feeling more than a little awkward or self-conscious. The bigger these negative feelings get, the less fun you're going to have.

If you're a woman, the effect can be an inability to achieve orgasm. It's difficult enough to be nude in front of somebody you scarcely know, but having a climax means truly giving up control. You can't do that if you're overwhelmed by feelings of doubt or fear or just plain awkwardness. You can't abandon yourself to passion if you don't feel safe with your partner. One result is that *he* may end up feeling inadequate. This is a less than ideal element to inject into a new relationship.

If you're a man, you may experience performance anxiety and difficulty in getting an erection, even though you're very attracted to the woman you're with. If you're too embarrassed to discuss it with her, to explain that you're merely nervous, the problem is compounded. She may feel you don't think she's attractive—and you know how sensitive women are about this matter.

In any case, what you are left with is a memory of an experience that is, at best, embarrassing, and at worst, can destroy your chances of building a good relationship. If the experience was frustrating, you're not going to want to take a chance on a repeat performance (or lack thereof). If it was embarrassing, you won't want to be confronted with someone who is a reminder of your discomfort.

And if you left your partner with either of you feeling even a little unsure about the experience, a whole new dynamic comes into play. Even if the sex was fantastic, it is normal to be more sensitized in that time right after you part company. ("Was I good? Did he/she really enjoy being with me? Did I make too much/too little noise?") The questions are endless, but they all are merely different ways of asking, *"Am I safe with this person?"* If you're not sure, you probably won't even call the person back, because you're afraid of what the answer might be.

The bottom line is that by having sex when you're not really ready, you can not only destroy the opportunity to build a wonderful relationship, but end up cheating yourself (and your partner) out of some really remarkable sex.

So, men *or* women, if you find that you have a tendency to become attracted to somebody on a physical level first, rein in those hormones and ask yourself where you are on the other two levels of attraction.

HONEY, IT AIN'T A RACE, AND IT DOESN'T WASH OFF LIKE MAKEUP!

I had an eye-opening experience a few months ago when I was sitting in on a business meeting. We were celebrating the fact that the sales force had just achieved their goals for the quarter and would receive a bonus.

As the champagne flowed, the talk turned to sex. Some of the women began a discussion about when to have sex with someone for the first time. Having worked with so many people and heard so many stories, I thought I'd heard everything, but I have to admit these women took me by surprise. Their approach to sex seemed very strategic and formulaic. One woman said, "Well, I always make sure that I *surprise* him when I'm going to do it." Another added, "I *always* have it by the fourth date." Other women made similarly calculating comments. Each seemed to have her own clear strategy planned out.

Not a word was uttered about whether or not they desired or loved a specific man, or if he was a good person for them; sex, for these women, had been reduced to a tactic for controlling or entrapping a man. If anybody harbored the notion that all women are starry-eyed romantics, this group would have shattered that notion forever.

The men, on the other hand, talked about seduction. They seemed to be focused on how quickly they could get a woman into bed, not on whether or not the woman was someone they truly cared for, or whether she was a person they *should* be in bed with. All they seemed to care about was how quickly they could score, and it seemed very much like a contest.

I'm not going to use this forum to moralize. I just want to say that I don't think any of the above motives can possibly lead to any sort of lasting happiness. As for "when to have sex," there's no perfect time or perfect date; that varies with the individuals involved (more on this in a little while). *The question you have to ask yourself is this: do you want to use sex as a strategy or a game or an ego boost—or do you want it to be an integral part of a loving relationship? The choice is yours.*

BEFORE IT'S ALL SHOWING, YOU'D BEST BE KNOWING: TOUGH QUESTIONS TO ANSWER WHILE YOU STILL HAVE YOUR CLOTHES ON

Ideally, the first sexual experience will occur spontaneously, when it is right for both individuals. We've discussed the reasons that having sex on the first few dates is probably very unwise, but in truth there is no categorically "right" date on which to have sex, no expressly "perfect" time for that first encounter. It's different for everybody.

So how do you know when the time and the person are right for *you*? I'm going to help you answer that question with some more questions. This is your first exercise for this chapter, and it is surely one of the most important exercises in the entire book. It's a list of questions that you really need to ask yourself—and you need to ask them *before* you find yourself naked with your new love. As usual, you may write your responses in the book or in your Relationship Journal.

If you are even remotely considering a sexual relationship with somebody, do not fail to do this exercise.

♥ ♥ ♥ ♡ ♥ ♥ ♥ ♥ ♥ ♥ ♥ ♥ ♥

Exercise 4-1. The Sex Questionnaire

❑ ***1. Have you handled the discussion of AIDS and other sexually transmitted diseases to your satisfaction? Have you discussed pregnancy and birth control (if applicable)? Have you each been tested for STDs? Will you use condoms?***

It's amazing to me how many couples, even in this day and age, *don't* talk about these life-threatening issues. Many people, particularly women, have said to me, "But it's so difficult talking about these things." I suggest to them that if they don't feel comfortable talking to their partner about safe sex, then they are not ready to have sex with that person.

Some people complain, "Talking about these things seems so calculating." Look, I'm the first to say sex should be spontaneous, but spontaneous does not mean foolish. *There are life-threatening issues to consider here.*

Perhaps you've decided, "I really don't think this person has been promiscuous. So I'm probably safe." Well, maybe the person *hasn't* been promiscuous. Maybe he or she has only had two sexual partners before you. But what if the first partner *was* highly promiscuous? What if the second partner was an intravenous drug user? Whether your potential lover is promiscuous isn't the question. *You have to feel safe about this before you enter into a sexual relationship with someone.*

Women often ask, "What if he won't have sex with me if I insist on covering all the bases about safe sex?" To which I reply, "If he doesn't care enough about you to respect your wishes in this area, I would ask you to consider that this is not a person you belong in bed with."

One woman asked me, "What do I do if he gives me a really good argument about why we don't need to be concerned about safe sex? I always give in so easily when someone gives me a convincing argument."

Let me tell you about something that happened to Joanne, a client of mine. "I was dating a man and we had reached the point where we were considering sex," Joanne related, "and naturally I brought up the issue of safe sex. Specifically, I wanted him to get tested for HIV. I had already been tested. Well, this man was giving me all sorts of arguments about why safe sex was a moot point. He happened to be a trial lawyer, and let me tell you, he was good. He made a powerful case. I knew I couldn't 'win' this debate. So I let him talk, and I listened, and when he was finished I said, 'You may be right. But it's my body, and as much as I care about you, under no circumstances am I going to compromise my health and safety.' Once he realized that this was a nonnegotiable point with me he had two options: either do it my way, or leave. Well, he didn't leave, and he eventually decided that I truly was right."

Joanne stood up for herself because she knows that *safe-sex practices should be nonnegotiable points.* (As should birth control.) My advice to you is to be as steadfast as Joanne; insist on any precautions you feel are necessary. Each person has to weigh her or his own options and come up with the best solutions. I am not going to recommend any one method because these are issues you must decide for yourself. But I will say this: with AIDS, in particular, my opinion is that *you cannot be too careful.*

Condoms are often touted as the safe-sex solution, but they are not foolproof. While latex condoms do offer a measure of protection (note, however, that studies have shown that the AIDS virus can penetrate lambskin condoms), the possibility of breakage should be considered. My recommendation is that the two of you discuss all the safe-sex issues—including (especially!) the results of your respective HIV tests. Again, you cannot be too careful.

By the way, I've been placing so much emphasis on AIDS in this discussion because it is life threatening, but that's not to give short shrift to the dangers of other sexually transmitted diseases. For example, hepatitis B is on the rise, and this disease can lead to cirrhosis of the liver or liver cancer. Furthermore, while herpes, chlamydia, and genital warts may not mean a death sentence, they can adversely affect the rest of your life, including all of your future relationships. Currently about 40 million Americans have some sort of sexually transmitted disease, and each year there are about 12 million new cases. Anyone who is *not* concerned about safe sex these days is in deep denial.

Besides engaging in honest dialogue with your partner, I recommend that you stay as informed as you possibly can about these matters; discuss them with your health care practitioner if you're comfortable doing so, and keep current on the latest health reports in the media. It seems researchers are making new discoveries about AIDS and other STDs virtually every week.

Now, before I get off my soapbox, in the interest of fairness, I have to point out that men are not the only "culprits" in avoiding safe-sex issues. Many women don't even bring the matter up in the first place—either because they automatically assume, without even asking, that their partner is going to be displeased, or because they themselves find such talk unpleasant. So I don't want anybody to think I'm trying to point the finger of blame at any one gender. Both parties are equally responsible for ensuring that they have safe sex.

There's a wealth of information out there on safe sex and pregnancy. Educate yourself, and discuss it with your partner *before* you get caught up in the heat of passion. If you don't feel comfortable discussing these topics with your partner, perhaps you should question why you *do* feel comfortable having sex with this person.

❑ ***2. Is this a person that you want to become more like?***

When you have sex you actually exchange more than body fluids, you exchange *energy*. As you become increasingly intimate with another person, aspects of your personalities begin to merge. You will, in ways both subtle and obvious, become more like the other person. *If you don't like the idea of becoming more like this person, keep the relationship nonsexual.*

❑ ***3. Is this a person whom you feel would be a suitable partner for your sister, brother, best friend, or (if they were the right age) your daughter or son?***

I had a good friend who had been in a two-year relationship with someone I really didn't think was very good for him. I asked him this question and he stopped dead and said, "You know, that's a *very* interesting question." He later told that me he had spent a lot of time pondering the matter, and that the answer he came up with finally helped him decide that this woman was not right for him. If your answer to this question is no, ask yourself, *if this person isn't good enough for someone you really care about, why is he or she good enough for you?*

❑ ***4. Is this a person whose company you could enjoy without having sex?***

For example, would you enjoy taking a trip with this person—driving, talking, shopping, taking a tour, spending fourteen hours a day together, relishing the companionship—if there were no sexual bond between you? Or would you get on each other's nerves after a day or so?

❑ ***5. Is this a person you would want to spend time with and have as a friend if you knew you would* never *have a sexual relationship?***

Use your answer to question 4 to help you with this one. Remember, although chemistry is important, chemistry alone will not make a relationship work.

❑ ***6. Do you feel intellectually attracted to, and emotionally safe with, this person?***

These are two different elements, both of which are necessary for a truly fulfilling sexual relationship. You want your sexual partner to be a person you truly like and respect, and whom you find intellectually stimulating. And you also want to feel that this person is someone with whom you can share your innermost thoughts and feelings, someone who will keep your confidences, someone with whom you are truly safe emotionally.

❑ ***7. Does this person appear to be free of the critical flaws detailed in chapter three?***

Please, please, *please* do not entertain becoming sexually bonded to anybody who has critical flaws or who, in any way, doesn't seem right for you. *You are not going to change this person,* and you could very well find yourself, years from now, trying desperately to get out of a hopeless entanglement.

❑ ***8. If it turned out that the two of you were sexually incompatible, could you discontinue the relationship with minimal emotional damage?***

What if, after having sex a few times, you began to feel that you'd made a mistake, that perhaps you weren't sexually compatible? I realize this requires a bit of speculation, but at this point in the relationship you should be able to make an educated guess. Do consider this possibility, because it could happen. Sometimes people have different sexual needs, or perhaps the chemistry just isn't there the way they'd hoped. Is this a person with whom you could discuss these issues openly, without emotionally devastating him or her? Equally important, do you feel you could handle this situation without becoming emotionally devastated yourself?

A cautionary note here: Don't jump to the conclusion that you're not sexually compatible just because it's not all fireworks the first few times. We'll discuss that further in the section that immediately follows this questionnaire.

❑ ***9. Do you feel protective toward this person and want to touch him or her in a tender as well as a passionate way?***

Are there some real emotional feelings, some regard for this person as a real human being? A truly intimate relationship is one that is suffused with tenderness as well as passion.

These are all important questions that you should be asking yourself, and merely by asking them, you will begin to gain a deeper understanding of what your own needs are. By answering them honestly, you will develop a clearer picture of what your prospective lover is like, and whether or not this person will meet more than your most insistent biological needs.

THE FIRST THREE TIMES DON'T COUNT

Once you've decided that the timing and the person are right, does this mean the first time the two of you have sex together it's going to be a sizzling experience for both of you? Probably not. In fact, the opposite may well be true.

That's perfectly normal. I have a theory that *the first three times you have sex with a person don't count.* They're like practice games before football season begins. Both people have a certain level of anxiety, and I think you should acknowledge that to each other. Tell your partner (and remind yourself) that the first three times don't count. You have no idea what a favor you'll be doing for your lover, and the pressure that you'll be taking off each other.

WHY THE TIMING OF "THE FIRST TIME" SHOULD BE THE WOMAN'S DECISION

When a woman has sex with somebody for the first time, it is, arguably, the only time she really has complete "control" over the act. After that, more than likely, her love for her man and her desire to fulfill his needs will lead her to have sex with him even on some occasions when it's really more his decision than hers. This is not to imply that a woman should never say no—for example, when she's not feeling well. But the truth is, many women do go out of their way to be accommodating to their partner's sex drive, and within the context of a loving relationship, there's absolutely nothing wrong with that. On that first time, however, it really is the woman who is in control.

This is as it should be; it's a way of evening things out, so to speak. For although in modern society women are achieving social, political, and economic equality with men, the physical reality of the sex act is that the male is unequivocally in a more "dominant" role. Because the woman has to literally open up and receive the man, she is in a more "submissive" role. Therefore, emotional safety is a much greater issue for her than it is for the man as they approach the sexual act.

A man should think about this when he is with a woman and realize that if he does not make that woman feel emotionally safe and comfortable with him, the sex is probably not going to be good for her—or for him, if her satisfaction matters to him at all.

BEING THE BEST LOVER YOU CAN BE

In a good relationship your sex life gets better and better, because you're growing more comfortable with each other all the time, and you are learning those special little things that your partner finds most exciting. It definitely helps, however, to have at least a basic level of technical ability before you even begin a relationship, so you'll have a general idea of how to please your partner.

But where are we supposed to have received this technical instruction? Did our parents really teach us? Did we learn anything of value about sexual technique in school? We really didn't (and if we had, the Board of Education and a horde of angry parents would probably have seen to it that our Sex Ed instructor never taught in that town again).

To be sure you are technically sexually educated, don't be afraid to do some research. There are plenty of manuals out there. So by all means educate yourself, if you need to, on the basics of sexuality and the anatomy of the opposite sex.

Now I have some information to share with you that I think will help you figure out what constitutes a good sexual experience for men and for women.

Of course, each of us is different and we each have our own likes and dislikes. Still, in sex as in virtually anything else, there are a few rules of thumb. For starters, there's an old saying that *in order to feel loved, men have to have sex, and in order to have sex, women have to feel loved.* There really is some truth to this generalization.

But let's get more specific. Recall chapter two, where we discussed men's and women's needs. These needs apply to sex as they do to other aspects of a relationship. Men, for example, need to feel adequate. They also frequently have a much harder time verbally expressing feelings than women do. When a man makes love to a woman (as opposed to merely having casual sex with her), to him that is a legitimate way of communicating with her. It's his way of showing her how he feels about her. If a woman rejects her man's sexual advances, he may think she is rejecting him as a person. He will not feel adequate.

For a woman to be truly satisfied sexually, all of her basic needs have to be met as well. For example, women need to feel emotionally secure, and they need to feel beautiful.

Granted, it can get pretty complicated trying to sort out and meet our own needs *and* the needs of our partner. It's worth the effort, however, because both people have to enjoy the sex for the relationship to work.

To help you understand your partner's, and your own, sexual needs a little better, I'm going to talk about men's and women's sexual turn-ons and turn-offs. These are not just arbitrary points, taken from the stated preferences of a few people. As in the items on the lists in previous chapters, these are the results of surveys taken during the time I owned my video dating service. We interviewed hundreds of men and women to find out what they looked for in a partner, what really turned them on and what raised a red flag and sent them running for the hills. The answers we got were almost universal.

THE TEN BIGGEST SEXUAL TURN-OFFS FOR MEN:

1. A sexually unresponsive woman. A man hates having sex with a woman who doesn't act as if she is enjoying having sex with him. The days when women were *expected* not to enjoy sex, when Queen Victoria advised her daughter to "just lie back and think of England," are long gone. Men are no longer happy with a woman who merely submits. Having sex with an unresponsive partner is like dancing alone; it's just not very satisfying, and it makes a man feel foolish. A man wants an active partner who enjoys having sex with him, and who lets him know that he's giving her pleasure.

2. A woman who never initiates sex. If a woman never initiates sex, the man doesn't feel wanted or desirable and, if he doesn't feel wanted or desirable, he probably isn't going to stick around. However, there is a big difference between *initiating* sex and *demanding* it. In fact if you're a woman you probably understand this distinction very well: think of the difference between a man who lets you know he *wants* you and a man who lets you know that he *expects* you to have sex with him. (Does the old word *duty* ring an ugly bell?)

3. A woman who doesn't take care of herself physically. Very simply, men are more visually driven creatures than women, and a woman's physical attractiveness is more important to them than a man's attractiveness is to most women. Generally speaking, a woman looks more for internal qualities, such as the attributes in a man that make her feel safe and secure. Does this mean you must look like a centerfold to attract a man? Of course not, but you should take care of yourself. You should try to be attractive in a pleasing, natural way by making the most of your physical attributes. This means using common sense about personal hygiene, and using cosmetics and clothing styles that accent your individual beauty instead of changing it. Eat right, exercise, and generally take good care of your body. Even a good haircut can work wonders for your attractiveness and self-image. You don't need to be obsessive about your looks (see the next item); just be conscious. Be the most attractive you can be.

4. A woman who is too concerned with her appearance. While men are turned on by a woman who is naturally pretty, they're very turned off by a woman who believes that physical beauty is all she has to offer. If a woman is obsessed with her appearance to the extent that she won't make love and abandon herself to orgasm because she's afraid it will smear her makeup, it shows she lacks the confidence that she has anything to offer but her looks. A confident woman simply doesn't dwell on her looks. She doesn't think about what she looks like during orgasm. A woman is going to be attractive to her man if her hair is messed up and her makeup is gone, so long as she is enjoying what she's doing with him. And, as we discussed in chapter three, most men don't like a lot of makeup, anyway. They don't *mind* makeup, but they don't want it to look as if they could touch your face and see their fingerprints.

5. A woman who doesn't enjoy giving a man oral sex. Oral sex is very important to men. A woman who doesn't enjoy oral sex, who doesn't treat the man's penis as if it's special, is rejecting a very significant part of him as a person. I cannot overstate the significance of oral sex to a man.

6. A woman who isn't sexually spontaneous. A man can be filled with desire for his woman at the oddest of times, perhaps at times when sex is the last thing on her mind. It is important to him that she be open and willing to accept his affections without some prescribed routine which must always be followed. If a woman requires a specific ritual and setting before she responds to her man's advances, she's telling him that the details are more important than his desire. By the same token, the man wants to feel his woman's desire for him arises spontaneously, too, and that she isn't afraid to act on it. Let's say one of you is washing the dishes when the other sneaks up from behind and makes an amorous gesture. Do you finish the dishes first . . . or put them aside and act on the impulse? Or perhaps you're out driving through the mountains, with nobody else around—and one of you feels a desire to stop and find a spot where you can spread a blanket and truly commune with nature. Do you keep driving till you find a motel, or do you act on the spontaneous desire? I think that at least some of the time you should *go for the spontaneity*. A man wants a woman to be able to respond to his—and her own—sexual desires.

7. A woman who acts as if sex is wrong or dirty. That's a big turn-off. Men want women who like sex just as much as they do. If a woman behaves as if sex is wrong or dirty, she is telling the man that, by extension, he is wrong and dirty for wanting it.

8. A woman who acts as if she's doing him a favor by having sex. For centuries, sex was the primary medium of exchange available to women. Women provided sex in exchange for security, approval, and power. The promise of the wedding night, replete with heretofore forbidden bliss, was undoubtedly the prime factor in many marriages. Today, women are discovering that sex is not their only form of currency, and those women who still try to use it as a medium of exchange are finding it is no longer a "seller's market." If a man senses that a woman is "doing him a favor" by having sex with him, it makes him feel as if he, as a person, isn't worthy of her desire. In his eyes, the emotional price for sex with her will simply be too high.

9. A woman who doesn't let a man know (in an attractive way) how to please her. If a woman wants a man to stop doing something *wrong*, she should encourage him to continue what he's doing *right*. If she tells him that she doesn't like what he is doing, to him it seems she is telling him that she doesn't like *him*. A better alternative would be to guide him to do something else she really enjoys. She can say, for example: "I like it better when you do this. It really turns me on." This way, she is getting what she wants, and he feels encouraged, rather than criticized. Both parties win. This isn't to say that *anyone* should compromise boundaries, or agree to anything that is personally objectionable or distasteful. Everyone has the right to firmly say, "No!" If you are with someone you wish to continue seeing, however, gentleness and diplomacy should *always* be your preferred course of action.

10. A woman who won't ever let her man give her oral sex. To a man, giving oral sex is a very loving act. When a woman doesn't ever allow him to do it, he thinks she is telling him that his love is unwelcome.

If you're self-conscious about being the recipient of oral sex, be assured that most men these days are very turned on by the taste and smell of a clean, healthy woman. They enjoy giving oral pleasure to the woman they love.

If a man is doing it in a way that you do not find pleasurable, refer to the instructions in number 9, above. If you just find oral sex uncomfortable physically, communicate that to your partner, letting him know that it isn't a problem with *him*. (A visit to the gynecologist may be appropriate, to address any physiological problems.)

If you are uncomfortable about oral sex for any reason, you should talk about it with your man. It always surprises me how many problems arise from unstated attitudes, and how frequently these problems are solved with just a little honest talk. What appears on the surface to be a major problem can often be the very vehicle that leads to greater intimacy and trust.

Those are the ten most prevalent turn-offs for men. Now, let's "clear the palate," if you will, and look at their ten biggest turn-ons.

THE TEN BIGGEST SEXUAL TURN-ONS FOR MEN:

1. A woman who really likes sex. Every man wants a responsive woman who enjoys making love with him.

2. A woman who initiates lovemaking from time to time. A man wants to know that his woman desires him as much as he desires her.

3. A woman who praises her man and makes him feel that he's the best lover in the world. A man wants to be with a woman who makes him feel that he's the paragon of sexual pleasure. She praises him, thanks him for her pleasure, and tells him how great he is. However, a woman should resist the temptation to pay false compliments, because the man will see right through it. She should, instead, focus on the wonderful ways he gives her pleasure, and let him know how terrific he makes her feel.

4. A woman who shares what turns her on in a positive, noncritical way. Because men are very sensitive, a positive message always works better than a negative one—and in the bedroom this is particularly true. Instead of saying, "Don't do this," say, "I like it even better when you do *this*," and gently guide him into doing what you like. You don't want to be a traffic cop or a choreographer in bed; you do want to be an enthusiastic, loving partner.

5. A woman for whom sex is just as much a priority as it is for her man. A man wants a woman who shares his desire for sex and lets him know that she is very attracted to him. Such a woman is a full partner to the man, and he thrives in that partnership.

6. A woman who is spontaneous and willing to have sex in new places, at unexpected times, and in different ways. Men like a sex life that's infused with spontaneity, imagination, and a sense of playfulness. If a woman remembers this, and acts accordingly, lovemaking will never get dull and routine.

7. A woman who really loves his penis and loves giving him oral sex. Don't worry about fancy techniques; if you really love his penis, and really love giving him oral sex, you will be "good" at it.

8. A woman willing to make love with the lights on. As you already know, most men are very visually oriented. I sometimes think the chief difference between men and women is that when it comes to lovemaking, women would choose candles and men would choose strobe lights. While a woman may want no lights or very muted lighting because she's worried about her physical flaws (a couple of extra pounds, a bit of cellulite), the man wants to see it *all*. A man is turned on by seeing his woman's body. The good news is that he's not going to be focused on those extra pounds; he's going to be focused on the fun the two of you are having. So . . . lighten up (so to speak)!

9. A woman who admires his body and lets him know it. Women have been the "sex objects" in our society for so long that we forget that men want to feel sexy and desirable, too.

10. A contented, happy, smiling woman. If his woman is really contented, a man is going to feel successful.

Okay, men, now it's your turn to discover what women don't and do like in the bedroom.

THE TEN BIGGEST SEXUAL TURN-OFFS FOR WOMEN:

1. A man who isn't educated sexually. He doesn't even know what, much less where, the clitoris is. Worse than that, he isn't interested in learning. See item number 2.

2. A man who isn't interested in learning how to more fully please a woman. Your partner will pick up on your lack of interest, and it will be a big turn-off for her. Every woman is different, and in sex, as in anything else, you never stop learning. No matter how much you know, there's always more to learn.

3. Boring sex. No variety: same time, same place, same position.

4. A man who is only interested in pleasing himself. If you want truly satisfying sex, learn what pleases your woman.

5. A man who doesn't listen or ask questions. See item number 2.

6. A man who is very goal-oriented, not pleasure-oriented. By this, I mean a man for whom sex is merely a means to achieve orgasm. Remember what we said in previous chapters about "enjoying the journey"? It definitely applies here too. Sometimes, getting there is all the fun!

7. A man who never gives his woman oral sex or manual sex. Straight intercourse just doesn't do it for many women. There are so many ways to please a woman; a good lover will want to explore them all.

8. A man who doesn't tell her she's beautiful in bed. One of the biggest emotional needs of a woman, as we discussed in chapter two, is to feel beautiful. It's also her *primary sexual need*, as we'll discuss in a moment. You have to make her feel beautiful in bed, because so much of her sexual response is dependent upon how she thinks you perceive her.

9. A man who doesn't tell her she's beautiful out of bed. See above. A woman wants to feel that you think she's beautiful all the time—not just in bed, but out of bed too. And if you don't make her feel beautiful out of bed, she's not going to want to be *in* bed with you.

10. A man with poor personal hygiene. Men should remember that if they want oral sex they need to be clean. If they want to be kissed, they need to brush their teeth. If personal hygiene is important on a date, it's even more important when you're in bed together.

Now here's what women *like*.

THE TEN BIGGEST SEXUAL TURN-ONS FOR WOMEN:

1. A man who is sexually educated about a woman's body. For instance, he *does* know what and where the clitoris is. He understands the subtle nuances of how (and where) to touch and caress her to fully arouse her desire.

2. A man who's pleasure-oriented, rather than goal-oriented. He isn't trying to hurry up and "do the deed," but rather is reveling in the sensual pleasure that comes from being with his woman. In other words, he has a "slow hand."

3. A man who makes her feel beautiful, in and out of the bedroom. He adores his woman all the time, and lets her *feel* his adoration.

4. A man who cares whether or not his partner is really satisfied. As in number 2 above, a woman wants a man who is completely involved in the process of giving and receiving pleasure, and is eager to know how he can increase the pleasure his partner feels. He is not so driven by his need to perform that he doesn't notice if his woman is responding. A sensitive man also realizes that no two women are alike, and that one woman's definition of satisfaction can change from day to day, depending upon her mood and the situation. While satisfaction for one woman may mean multiple, screaming orgasms, for another (or for the same woman, at another time) it may mean the sweetness of afterglow when she knows she has brought *him* pleasure. He asks what pleases her right now, and tries to give it to her.

5. A man who makes her feel that she is a priority to him. She doesn't need to be the *only* factor in his life, but she does need to be a *very important* factor.

6. A man who makes her feel uniquely desired for herself, not just because she's an available outlet for his lust. She needs to feel *special*, not merely *convenient*.

7. A man who touches her and compliments her when they are not in bed. This ties in closely with number 6. A woman needs to feel appreciated by her man even when he's not in the throes of sexual desire.

8. A man with good hygiene. A woman in love literally devours her man with all her senses. He should present himself to her in the most appealing way possible, so that he looks, sounds, feels, smells, and tastes fresh, clean, and delicious.

9. A man who realizes that, for her, the time after sex is just as important. So often, men deprive themselves and their partners of the exquisite, shared tenderness of afterglow. You could write volumes about the "whys," but we won't get into that here. Just take a few minutes to hold her. You'll never regret it.

10. A man who realizes that she likes to have orgasms by means other than intercourse, too. In fact, many women have trouble reaching orgasm through intercourse alone; it's mostly a matter of simple physiology. A woman must feel it's safe to be honest about her needs. For the man's part, he should be as inventive, creative, and spontaneous as he wants *her* to be. While it's true that intercourse is wonderful, and can be just as pleasurable for a woman as for a man, it's also true that God gave men ten fingers, ten toes, lips, a tongue, and a job to earn enough money to buy a shower massage. You figure it out!

GETTING TO THE CORE: THE PRIMARY SEXUAL NEEDS OF MEN AND WOMEN

Beyond the turn-offs and turn-ons we've just finished discussing, men and women have basic primary sexual needs. How can a man meet that need for a woman, and vice versa? Since women do establish the level of happiness in a relationship, I'm going to start with a woman's primary sexual need.

Men, I'm assuming that your relationship makes your woman feel loved, cared for, and understood, that it meets all of the needs described in chapter two. I'm further assuming that you're doing your best to avoid the ten sexual turn-offs described earlier, while trying your best to observe the ten turn-ons.

Now I'm going to share a secret with you about a woman's primary need in the bedroom. If you remember nothing else about her sexual needs, remember this:

The primary need that a woman has during lovemaking is to feel beautiful and desired by her man.

As we discussed in chapter two, a man seems to have little problem with making a woman feel beautiful and desired at the beginning of a relationship, when he is filled with that hunt-and-conquer energy. Many men are much better at *getting* what they want than at *keeping* it.

If, however, you don't meet your woman's primary need throughout the course of the relationship, she may very well figure out a way to get it filled elsewhere. Maybe she will flirt at work, or have an affair, or even leave you for another man. At any rate, she will start to lose her glow, that sparkle in her eye, the smile on her face, the spring in her walk, and all those other little things that mark her as a woman in love. Women don't get dull and unattractive from lack of love, but rather from lack of the kind of attention it takes to make them feel desirable and sexy. To keep your woman happy and beautiful, you must make her *feel* beautiful, and not just when you want to make love. How do you do this? There are many ways, but this will give you the basic idea: *Take time to look at her, to really notice how beautiful she is, and let her know.*

Whatever part of her body you admire, tell her. If it's her legs, tell her how lovely they are, and caress them with your eyes as well as your fingertips. Tell her you think about her long legs on the way to work, and that you have a tough time concentrating because the image so fills your mind. Tell her you love her mouth, that it's the sexiest mouth in the world, and then kiss it passionately. Let your words reflect the passion in your heart, and let your actions mirror your words. Even if she thinks she's overweight, look at her body and share with her the beauty you see. If her breasts are small and you *love* pert little breasts, tell her and then *show* her. Let her see and hear that you feel like the luckiest man in the world. Remember, this is the one woman you've chosen to make love to (and in this day and age *it should only be one at a time*). Make her feel beautiful and desired. Tell her no one has ever filled your thoughts and made you feel the way she does.

If you're not in a relationship, or if you're in a relationship that's lost its spark and sizzle, take a lesson from couples who are obviously, demonstrably in love. Look at them and watch how they interact. They interact as if there's no one else in the room. If Julia Roberts walked in, arm-in-arm with Brad Pitt, neither of them would even notice. That's how you want to make your woman feel: you want to make her feel she is so lovely that even if the most gorgeous actress or supermodel in the world walked into the room, you would never notice. If a man sees his woman as beautiful, she *is* beautiful. And she will be much more likely to meet your primary sexual need (see page 150). Women thrive in a reciprocal love relationship.

After all, if this is *the* woman, *your* woman, it is your job to make her feel beautiful and desired. Don't do it halfway, and for goodness sake don't leave it undone. If you do, she'll either leave you or put a low ceiling on the happiness of the relationship. If, on the other hand, you make your woman feel beautiful and desired, she will make your life heaven on earth.

Now let's talk about a man's primary need in bed. Very simply, it is this:

The primary need that a man has during lovemaking is to feel as if he is the best lover his woman has ever had.

Whereas a woman wants to feel desirable, a man wants to feel that there is nobody who can "perform" like him. Performance is, after all, the measure of a man's sense of self-worth. And how can his woman make him feel like the great lover he wants to be? The truth is, we women have a pretty good deal going on here. We can meet a man's primary sexual need by being satisfied, by getting *our* needs met in bed.

We have only to do it in an attractive way. We let him know what makes us happy. And when he does something that makes us happy, we let him know about it. We tell him, not just in bed, but at other times, too. Maybe we lean over at dinner and whisper in his ear, "My God, you were incredible last night. You make me so happy. I'm the luckiest woman I know." Your man needs to feel he is completely satisfying you. He wants to please you.

A man also likes it when you come up with little fantasies for the two of you to act out. When you give him ideas about things he can do to please you, and praise him when he does them, he feels like a winner.

Never forget to put a positive spin on everything you communicate to him in the bedroom. Let's say he wasn't giving you oral sex very much in the beginning of your relationship, but has been doing it more often lately. Don't convey an attitude of, *It's about time.* Instead, just tell him he's doing it better than ever before. If there's something you want him to do differently, gently guide him where you want him, and then compliment him for doing it so well.

Men also want you to respond, whether with moans, groans,

words, movement or, preferably, all the above! They need to know if they're "on target," if what they're doing is really the right thing to totally satisfy you. It is definitely in a woman's interest to let a man know how she feels.

It's up to you to make your man feel that he's the greatest lover in the world.

HOW YOU CAN MAKE SURE SEX JUST KEEPS GETTING BETTER

The longer your sexual relationship goes on the better it should be. Sex is, after all, a form of communication that is at once sublime and intense. It is the way two people communicate their feelings of love to each other. In order for it to be good and keep getting better, you must:

1. *Concentrate on the other person,* so that the feeling, in both your minds, is that nobody else exists in your shared universe at this moment.
2. *Crave the other person,* hunger so deeply for this person that you ache, and let the person know it.
3. *Totally lose control.* The only way to have an orgasm is to lose control. But in a general sense as well, you have to let your defenses down; you have to be willing to give yourself completely to the other person.

Take a pinch of atmosphere . . .

Now that we've gotten the list of "musts" out of the way, we can look at a "should." There should be a primary place where you make love, usually the bedroom. It shouldn't be the only place, but it should be the main place, and it should be a true haven.

It should also be attractive to all the senses, because different people are attracted on different levels. As we briefly discussed in chapter three, some people are visually oriented, some people are auditory, some are excited by touch. And we didn't even mention taste or smell. . . . There are some folks who are attracted on all these levels but, for most of us, one or two elements are predominant.

So your job is to pay attention to the details: specifically, to be aware of your levels and, most important, your partner's levels of attraction—and then to fashion your "love nest" accordingly.

1. *Smell is important.* Scented candles can be wonderful, as can fresh-cut flowers or incense.
2. *Lighting is important.* Soft lighting can help establish a romantic ambience, while a brightly lit room can really excite someone who is very visually inclined.
3. *Tactile sensations are important.* Buy and use sheets that really feel good to the touch, such as high thread-count cotton, or satin or silk if you feel extravagant and can afford them. I personally believe that spending money on exquisite sheets is a wise investment. Save money in other places; you're going to use those sheets for years.
4. *Romantic music is great, particularly for someone who is attracted on an auditory level.* Select music that says, even without words, what is in your heart.
5. *Taste is a factor that is sometimes forgotten when talking about romance.* But don't overlook the possibilities here; a box of champagne truffles or the occasional bottle of fine wine can add a delightful element of sensuality to your little haven.
6. *Overall atmosphere is important.* Ask yourself if everything in the room is a reflection of your sensuality and your partner's. If not, get busy and make it so.

The point is to indulge your senses and those of your partner. Sensuality is very important to a truly fulfilling sex life, and, in my opinion, to a full enjoyment of life in general.

. . . Stir in a bit of spontaneity . . .

Atmosphere is important to women in particular, but women should remember that men, on the other hand, really love spontaneity. So, if your man makes the effort to provide you with romantic atmosphere, you should do your best to "let your hair down," and really go with the sensuality you feel. The old adage about a man wanting "a lady in the parlor and a whore in bed" isn't far off the mark, though he's quite as likely to be looking to the parlor with a gleam in his eye, too!

. . . And add a little exercise . . .

Yes, you do have a few more assignments (three more, to be exact), but they're fun. Do complete them before going on to the next chapter. For the written exercises, as in previous chapters, you may write in the space I've provided in this book, or you can set up pages in your Relationship Journal.

♥ ♥ ♡ ♥ ♥ ♥ ♥ ♥ ♥ ♥ ♥ ♥ ♥

EXERCISE 4-2. DECIDING HOW YOU CAN MEET YOUR PARTNER'S NEEDS IN THE BEDROOM

In chapter two we talked about the top seven needs of men and women in a relationship. Most, if not all, of these needs can be applied to a sexual situation. For your convenience, I am repeating the lists here (if you need more details, refer to the explanations in chapter two). Study the lists and then write down one way that you could meet each one of your partner's needs during a sexual experience.

The Top Seven Needs of a Woman:	*The Top Seven Needs of a Man:*
1. Emotional security	1. To feel adequate just the way he is
2. To feel that she is a priority in her man's life	2. To feel he is in charge
3. Attention	3. To feel admired and respected

4. To feel cherished	4. To have his woman as his confidante
5. To be listened to	5. Companionship
6. Affection and romance	6. To feel appreciated
7. For her man to embrace her goals	7. To feel sexually fulfilled

My partner's seven basic needs, and how I can meet them in the bedroom

Need 1:____

____

How I can meet that need in the bedroom:____________

____

____

Need 2:____

____

____

How I can meet that need in the bedroom:____________

____

____

Need 3:____

____

How I can meet that need in the bedroom:____________

____

____

Need 4:____

____

How I can meet that need in the bedroom:__________________

____

____

Need 5:____

____

How I can meet that need in the bedroom:__________________

____

____

Need 6:____

____

How I can meet that need in the bedroom:__________________

____

____

Need 7:____

____

How I can meet that need in the bedroom:__________________

____

____

♥ ♥ ♥ ♡ ♥ ♥ ♥ ♥ ♥ ♥ ♥ ♥ ♥

Exercise 4-3. Continuing Education

This isn't a brief exercise but a longer-term project. Your "assignment" is to become as educated about sexuality as you can. Here are a few books on the subject that I recommend.

- *The Complete Guide to Safer Sex* by the Institute for Advanced Study of Human Sexuality
- *Hot Monogamy* by Dr. Patricia Love and Jo Robinson
- *What Men Really Want: Straight Talk From Men About Sex* by Susan Crain Bakos
- *The Guide to Getting It On!: A New and Mostly Wonderful Book About Sex for Adults of All Ages* by The Goofy Foot Press
- *The Art of Sexual Ecstasy* by Margo Anand
- *Secrets About Men Every Woman Should Know* by Barbara DeAngelis
- *The New Joy of Sex* by Alex Comfort
- *Anne Hooper's Pocket Sex Guide* by Anne Hooper
- *How to Satisfy a Woman Every Time and Have Her Beg For More* by Naura Hayden
- *The One-Hour Orgasm* by Dr. Bob Schwartz
- *How to Drive Your Man Wild in Bed* by Graham Masterson
- *Sex on Campus: The Naked Truth About the Real Sex Lives of College Students* by Leland Elliott and Cynthia Brantley
- *Mindblowing Sex in the Real World* by Sari Locker
- *The Best Love, The Best Sex: Creating Sensual, Soulful, Supersatisfying Relationships* by Suzi Landolphi
- *For Each Other: Sharing Sensual Intimacy* by Lonnie Barbach, Ph.D.
- *365 Ways to Improve Your Sex Life* by James R. Petersen

There are many other excellent books and tapes as well. A browse through the "sexuality" section of your local bookstore will show you there's plenty of information available on this subject.

♥ ♥ ♥ ♥ ♡ ♥ ♥ ♥ ♥ ♥ ♥ ♥ ♥

Exercise 4-4. Make Yourself Sexy

Do everything you can (and anything you need) to make yourself feel sexy. If you're a woman, take a bubble bath. If you're a man, pump iron or whatever it is that makes you feel sexier. Do whatever it takes—within the bounds of reason, good sense, and local, state, and federal statutes—to make you radiate sexual confidence from within. Wear this confidence like a suit of fine clothing when you meet your partner.

Your assignment is to list five things you plan to do to build that sexual confidence:

I plan to

1. ______________________________

____

2. ______________________________

____

3. ______________________________

____

4. ______________________________

____

5. ______________________________

____

I also suggest that you go over the questionnaire that appeared earlier in this chapter, and then go back and review the questions you've asked yourself in previous chapters. Really reflect on your answers. This way, you will have a better understanding of your needs and your prospective partner's needs. You will be more prepared when your relationship reaches the point where you're ready to act on the chemistry you feel.

We know that sex is very important, and that it's going to get better and better as you and your partner learn and understand more about each other.

♥ The Fifth Principle ♥

Conviction

Conviction is the process of becoming convinced that the person you are dating is someone with whom you want to enter into a higher level of commitment. This stage of the relationship is a time of significant change, and many fears and doubts may come up as you search for the answer to that all-important question: Where is this relationship going?

If you've assimilated the information from chapter four, you have a good working knowledge of the sexual turn-ons and turn-offs that make an intimate relationship work or not work. If you've decided to enter into a sexual relationship, I hope you've chosen your sexual partner with care and that the sex you're having is getting better and better all the time.

Now it's time to talk about *Conviction*. Here the plot really starts to thicken; by this stage of the relationship, you are becoming convinced that this is the person for you. You don't decide this all at once, of course. It happens in steps and is rarely a smooth progression. This is the precommitment phase, and it is a critical time because the decisions you make now could literally mean the difference between a lifetime of happiness and one of disappointment. That's why this chapter contains more questionnaires and checklists than previous chapters. You need to have at your disposal every possible tool to help you make one of the most important decisions of your life.

IF IT DOESN'T KILL US, IT WILL MAKE US STRONGER: NAVIGATING "THE SWITCH"

Sue first met Rob at a church social. Conversation between them was easy, as they shared many interests and values. The mutual attraction they felt was powerful and obvious. They began seeing each other almost daily, sharing all their free moments. Rob was very attentive, considerate, and romantic to a fault. When they eventually found themselves in bed, it was delightfully intense.

After a couple of months, however, something changed. Rob suddenly became less available to Sue than he had previously been. He often had other plans that prevented them from being together. While he felt that his reasons were all perfectly legitimate, she felt he was avoiding her. She began calling him whenever he was conspicuously absent. He, in turn, became even more elusive, and Sue felt abandoned. She felt hurt, used, and angry.

Does this sound familiar? I'd be surprised if you said no. Though each relationship is as unique as the individuals in it, virtually all relationships go through similar phases. What Rob and Sue experienced is in fact quite common.

The early, presexual stage of a romantic relationship is characterized by a process called "the pursuit": one person is pursuing, or romancing, the other. Traditionally the man was the pursuer, and the woman the pursued; these days, however, the old roles and rules are blurring, and quite often the woman is the one who does the chasing. No matter who's in pursuit, the dynamics of the relationship change once the two people become sexually involved.

Let's imagine you're in a relationship that has progressed to the point where the two of you have become physically intimate and are growing closer emotionally as well. You are now totally enthralled with each other, in a state of absolute infatuation—just like Rob and Sue in the example above.

What happens next? Do you decide you were made for each other, head for the altar, and live happily ever after? If only it were that easy. What usually happens is the strange and often disturbing phenomenon I've just described. Judith Sills, in her insightful book *A Fine Romance*, calls this phenomenon "the switch."

What exactly is the switch? It's a role reversal of sorts, and here's how it comes about. After those first few weeks or months of being in a relationship, you're in the infatuation stage—you're totally in love, you're crazy about each other, you can't keep your hands off each other. Then all of a sudden *fear sets in* for either one or both of you. That is when, and why, the switch happens. What generally happens is that the original pursuer starts to back off, and the person who was pursued feels very anxious and begins to do the pursuing, trying to "hang on" to something new and wonderful.

The switch is not necessarily a one-time occurrence within the relationship. Sometimes the roles change back and forth several times so it's really never clear who pursued whom. But ultimately that's not the important issue. What is important is that *both* people understand the switch and its significance to the future of the relationship.

The switch is a critical event, or series of events, that can make or break the relationship. If one of the partners never had the intention of carrying through to commitment, the switch will usually be the end of the relationship.

It isn't my intention to pick on men, but more often than not, it is the man who initiates the switch. In a worst-case, but by no means universal, scenario, the man may have had no intention of commitment and may have been only seeking sexual gratification, or an ego boost, or the sheer pleasure of the chase. When the switch happens, that man is not only going to back off quickly, he's going to be "outta there." As heartbreaking as this may be for you if you're the woman in this situation, your best option is to just let him go, because he's definitely not the person for you. You don't have the right or the power to change him, and you shouldn't waste your time and energy trying.

Granted, it's not always the man who doesn't want a committed relationship. Sometimes the woman was just in it for fun, or for validation of her attractiveness, or for the novelty of a new love. Once the newness wears off and the switch happens, *she's* going to be gone. My advice to you men who find yourselves in this predicament is the same as to women: Don't waste your time trying to change that woman into your soul mate. You can't do it.

What frequently adds to the sense of desperation you experience when faced with the switch is you forget that *you cannot be so attached to the outcome of a relationship that you are unable to let go when the relationship has reached a dead end.* There are other people out there with whom you can develop a relationship naturally, without anything being forced. If a relationship just isn't working, *let it go*, and make room in your life for one that does work.

What about couples in which both the man and the woman truly want a lasting relationship—are they immune from the switch? Not at all; more than likely the switch will occur anyway, following that delightful period of being totally, madly in love. Richard Bach, in his book *A Bridge Across Forever*, describes this transition as "the end of the beginning," as opposed to "the beginning of the end." I want to add that having a great sexual relationship is no safeguard against the switch. Ironically enough, *the better the sex, the more likely it is that the switch will happen.*

What can a couple do to ensure that their relationship survives the switch? First, accept the switch as a normal part of the relationship process. Don't take it personally; it isn't just you. Second, recognize that *fear* is the reason behind the switch, and *some fear is very normal for both men and women at this point in the relationship.* In fact, I'd be a lot more concerned about someone who had no fears. After all, you are approaching a decision which could well affect the rest of your life. This decision should be approached with clarity and, yes, even some apprehension. Third, try to understand what the switch really is, and what it is saying about you, your partner, and the process of your relationship.

To better understand the switch, let's look more closely at it. It generally takes one of two forms, the *retreat* or the *stalemate.*

Form 1: The Retreat

During the retreat, the person who was the pursuer suddenly begins to back off; it's somewhat akin to slamming down hard on the brakes. The first sign you may notice is that your partner is starting to behave in ways that are not consistent with previous behavior. The situation between Rob and Sue is a good example of a retreat.

Other signs of change may also be apparent; perhaps the flow of compliments, once freely and honestly given, has diminished to a trickle, or worse, has deteriorated into frequent criticism (more on that in a moment). Or perhaps those once-frequent references to the future are now going conspicuously unstated. Any of these occurrences can be very puzzling and disturbing, but they're all reactions to fear.

Some of these fears may seem irrational. One or both partners may feel as if they are losing a part of their individual identity, their autonomy, and their sense of independence. They may perceive a threat of entrapment. Of course these fears are groundless if the relationship is a good one that offers both parties room to grow. But it may be difficult for somebody who's in the throes of "relationship panic" to understand this.

It's not at all uncommon for the fearful person to become hypercritical of the partner at this stage. While this can be distressing to you if you're on the receiving end of the criticism, please know it's normal. Anything your partner perceives as negative about you or the relationship will become much more acute in his or her mind. Your partner may exaggerate these perceived faults for one reason: to rationalize the need to run away if necessary. Sadly, at this point many people do indeed run.

Form 2: The Stalemate

The switch can also take a less blatant form called the stalemate. In a stalemate, the signals are considerably more subtle. Instead of bringing the relationship to an abrupt end, the stalemate usually involves an attempt to freeze it right where it is, because that's where the person is comfortable. The person who's trying to stalemate usually has a rationalization for doing so. I've worked with many couples whose relationships illustrated this phenomenon.

Myra and Sam had been dating for months, but when the relationship began to turn serious, Sam decided he wanted to get his graduate degree before making any heavy decisions—so suddenly all talk about the future was off. Nick and Sara were also approaching the conviction stage in their relationship, when Nick stalemated with the rationalization that he wanted to reach a higher income level before making a commitment to Sara. In the case of Lynnette and Charles, it was Lynnette who initiated the stalemate. She still had children in high school, and she decided she wanted to hold off any decision about the future until the youngest was off to college.

In all of these cases, what was really happening was that the person who had been the pursuer became nervous, took a step back, and actually tried to freeze the relationship just as it was, halting the normal progression, the natural flow of getting closer.

We already know that the stalemate tactic won't work. We either get better or we get worse, but we don't stay the same—and that goes for relationships, too. Change is just a part of life. Of the three couples above, only Nick and Sara were able to work through the stalemate and carry their relationship through to the commitment stage. The stalemating partners in the other two couples did not choose to face up to their fears, and eventually their partners left them.

Whichever form the switch takes—retreat or stalemate—it generally happens two to nine months after the relationship becomes sexual. Though the switch can be a time of upheaval, you can turn it to your advantage if you

- understand it better and react to it with compassion—for yourself and your partner—instead of fear.
- maintain confidence in your ability to be okay even if the relationship does not work out.

You now have a general idea of what the switch is and why it occurs, but you may also need to take a closer look at exactly what the switch is telling you about yourself, your partner, and your relationship.

ORDINARY COLD FEET, OR TRUE COMMITMENT-PHOBIA? TAKE THIS TEST AND FIND OUT

We've established that some fear is natural at this point in the relationship. The switch may well be merely a reaction to these normal fears. On the other hand, the switch can signal a real fear of commitment, a deep internal problem.

How can you tell if you just have cold feet or a full-blown case of commitment-phobia? If you examine your past patterns, you'll probably find the answer. Here are a few questions to ask yourself:

1. Do you have a pattern of dating a person, becoming very picky after a couple of months, and "discarding" that person? Have you done this time after time?
2. Does your romantic interest tend to evaporate in three or four months?
3. Do you always date more than one person at a time?
4. Do you tend to become involved with people who are unavailable emotionally, or perhaps married, or in some other way unsuitable partners?
5. When you start a relationship, do you start it with an escape hatch (e.g., "She's great, but she's too young," "He's wonderful, but he's too old")?

If you answered "always" (or even "frequently") to any of the above, it may not be the normal switch that is occurring. *You may truly have an internal problem with commitment.* This could keep you from ever getting the relationship you want.

The exercise that follows may help you clarify these matters.

♥ ♥ ♥ ♥ ♥ ♡ ♥ ♥ ♥ ♥ ♥ ♥ ♥

EXERCISE 5-1. LONG-TERM VS. SHORT-TERM RELATIONSHIPS

Review the questions above, and think about the relationships you've had. Determine how many relationships have lasted for a year or more, and how many lasted for ninety days or less.

- ONE YEAR PLUS: ________________________________
- NINETY DAYS OR LESS: ____________________________

If you've had many short-term relationships and few or no long-term ones, more than likely that's due to one of two reasons:

1. *You're letting sex happen too quickly.* Having sex too soon can short-circuit even a potentially wonderful relationship. See chapter four for guidelines on the timing of sex.
2. *You have a real fear of commitment.* Many people do; we'll address that in the next chapter.

Since we can reasonably assume that the switch is going to occur in some form no matter what, is there anything that can be done about it? Yes, there is, and that's what we're going to talk about now. If you sense intuitively that your partner is backing off, you're probably right, but there are several things you can do.

1. You can just ignore the unusual behavior and very possibly, it will go away. Time will heal it.
2. You can question the person about it. Some people can confront their fears very easily, and they respond quite well to talking about the problem.
3. You can get angry or upset. Warning: generally, that resolves nothing; it only causes the person to become more fearful and perhaps back off even more.
4. You can strike back. You can become completely unavailable, very busy, perhaps begin to see other people. That, too, could backfire; the person might just let you go. Besides, striking back constitutes game-playing, and has no place in a real relationship.
5. You can have The Big Relationship Conversation, in which you ask or demand to know, "Where is this relationship going?"

The best recommendation is that you *do* have some sort of conversation, but not "The Big One." Simply express your feelings as honestly and clearly as you are able, and if the other person gives you an ambivalent response, *don't fall apart.* Just back off a little bit. Draw upon the self-confidence you've been building. *Try to establish a healthy detachment from the outcome of this relationship.*

It's perfectly all right to become a *little* less available yourself. This doesn't mean you refuse to answer the person's phone calls or that you run off to Aruba with someone else. Just stop expressing your interest so dramatically. Keep in mind that you're not doing this as a strategy or a manipulative tactic; you're merely engaging in self-protection. Take care of *you*; concentrate a little bit more on your work or a hobby or your personal growth.

I know it's very scary to back off, because you're afraid you're going to lose the relationship. You're afraid that if you're busy the person will never ask you out again. If that does happen, however, you haven't really lost anything but the *illusion* of a good relationship. *If the relationship is truly a good one, you will get through this stage.*

A real internal shift must occur when a person is in the process of becoming convinced that you're the "right" one. The decision to make a commitment is a highly individual matter, and each person has to do it in his or her own way. *You cannot make another person do anything. People are going to do what they are going to do.*

You are the single best insurance that you are going to end up with a good relationship. You are the one who makes this choice by doing what's right for yourself, and by always conducting yourself in a way that shows you have integrity and honesty.

If you understand the switch and know how to navigate it, you will do what is right for yourself and the other person. The very good news is that if your relationship survives the switch, you'll both come out of it stronger and more sure of yourselves as a couple.

WE SURVIVED THE SWITCH . . . NOW WHAT?

Let's say you've gotten past the switch. You've explored your respective fears and determined that they're pretty normal; there are no deep relationship phobias at work, and the two of you want to continue as a couple. Generally what happens, once you've navigated the switch, is that you have both become physically and emotionally comfortable together. You've begun to take for granted that you're going to spend Saturday nights together. People have started to ask you out as a couple. You're "an item."

Now you're really getting into the conviction phase. You've reached the stage of trying to decide whether or not this is the right person for you. You're in the process of being convinced that this is (or is not) a person with whom you might have a future.

At this stage two decisions must be made:

1. You must decide if this is a person with whom you want to have a higher level of commitment. However your decision manifests itself—marriage, or living together, or just spending the next two or three years together—you are going to have to decide if this person is right for you.
2. Your partner has to decide the same about you.

And that's really the crux of this chapter: how to come to this decision. What we're discussing applies no matter what your idea of high-level commitment is—whether or not you want to get married or just move in together.

HOW LONG SHOULD THIS CONVICTION PHASE LAST?

One of the most frequent questions I'm asked is, "How long should you date a person before you decide whether or not he [or she] is the one?" And the answer I inevitably give is this: *The younger you are, the longer you should take.* Why? The younger you are, the less time you have spent learning about and understanding yourself and your needs. Your tastes and lifestyle are more likely to change.

Of course, no matter how old you are, your needs are still going to shift from time to time, as life is all about growth and change. If you're younger, however, most of the significant shifts are still ahead of you. You will, in many ways, be a completely different person at thirty-nine than you are at nineteen. Many relationships simply do not survive the major life shifts we all go through.

Even if you're a very mature person who really feels you know yourself and what you want in a partner, my recommendation is this: *the minimum time you should spend with a person before making any high-level commitment is twelve months.* Everyone is different, but *on the average, you should take between twelve and twenty-four months before you make a major decision.*

On the other hand, it's possible to take *too* long, and I believe you should spend no longer than twelve to eighteen months with an individual who does not indicate that he or she is at least *contemplating* having a serious relationship and a future with you. Otherwise, if what you want is a serious relationship and that's not what the other person wants, it will be comparable to putting all of your money in a bank but never being able to make a withdrawal. Nobody wants to do that.

By the same token, neither do you want to consider the time you've spent in a relationship that ended as "wasted" time. If you have truly enjoyed the time you spent with that person, if you've made a life together—for however brief a period—and you've built great memories, you have spent your time well.

I don't know about you, but I think it's very unattractive to hear a person say, "I wasted a year of my life on that relationship." A much healthier attitude is one such as country singer Ronnie Milsap expressed in a song a few years ago: "I wouldn't have missed it for the world." It's understandable that you might feel a bit of sadness or regret about how the relationship turned out (or didn't turn out), but if you had a good year with that person, and benefited in any way, *you did not waste a year of your life.*

COMPATIBILITY, NOT SEX, IS THE KEY

A big part of this chapter is going to be dedicated to the subject of *compatibility*. And the truth is:

Most relationships don't end because the two people are not in love; they end because the two are not COMPATIBLE.

Right on the heels of this basic truth is yet another one, which you should burn into your memory:

Good sex, great sex, even FABULOUS *sex, does not equal compatibility!*

Think of it this way: sex takes up a very *important part* of our time, but a very *minuscule portion* of our time compared with the rest of our life. No matter how wonderful the sex is, if the two of you are not truly compatible in other fundamental ways you do not have a good foundation for a lasting relationship.

COUPLEHOOD: MAKING IT REAL

Let's say you've gotten past the starry-eyed stage, but have you really experienced life as a couple? I strongly suggest you not even consider making any serious decisions about your future until you can answer "yes" to all of the questions that follow.

1. ***Are you a couple to yourselves and to the world?*** This is the first and perhaps most obvious consideration. You should be routinely spending time together as a couple. Not only that, but your friends should be inviting the two of you out as a couple.

2. ***Are you spending a lot of unstructured time together?*** You should be able to spend lots of time together without any particular plan—going to the grocery store, watching TV, or reading. Your "together time" should no longer have to center around a specific event. It's very important to know that this is a person you can just *be* with.

3. ***Do you spend holidays together?*** Ideally, you've had a chance to spend *all* holidays together before you make a commitment. Holidays can be hectic and stressful as well as joyous; it's important to know how the two of you share these experiences.

4. ***Have you met your partner's family (and has your partner met yours)?*** All people are affected by their families differently, but the fact is, our families do influence us profoundly. To see where your partner came from is to know a great deal about

who this person is. You will gain information that will help you understand him or her much better.

5. Have you seen each other sick, even if it's only been with the flu or a cold? We all get ill at one time or another. You need to experience how your relationship works during such an inherently stressful period.

6. Have you experienced some sort of a crisis together? It's important to know that you can support each other through crises, whether the crisis be in your work, other relationships, as a result of an illness, or some other significant event.

7. Have you had conflict, and were you able to resolve it? You cannot be close to an individual and never feel anger. It's how you resolve the conflict that counts, not whether or not you have it. We'll talk more about conflict later in this chapter.

You have not been intimate with a person if you've never been angry with that person.

8. Have you taken a trip together? Taking a trip with a person for the first time can be a real eye-opener. I recommend that you take at least a weekend trip together, but if you can afford it, a week-long trip is better. It doesn't have to be a trek to some exotic resort; even a camping trip will do.

Why is taking a trip such a litmus test? If a single holiday can be stressful, it's nothing compared to a vacation. You might be surprised how many relationships fall apart on vacation. When I owned the video dating service, people would come in so many times and tell me, "I've fallen madly in love; we're going to go off on vacation to Mexico." Then they would come back and say, "Take me off of 'hold'—I want to start dating again. That's the craziest person I've ever met. He [or she] drove me nuts."

Few experiences will test a relationship more than being in a confined space such as a hotel room, or worse yet, *really* having to travel. You haven't truly been with a person until you've spent hours in a car together, going from one location to another, changing hotels, packing up, moving. A week away with a person in confined quarters can be very stressful, and can reveal much about that person, about yourself, and about how you're really going to be as a couple.

There's no way that anyone can go on a long trip and not, at some point during the heavy travel schedule, get tired or hungry or irritable. During those times, pay close attention to how (or if) you resolve conflicts, whether or not you're able to just pass them off, go on with the trip, and make it a magical time.

Observe, also, how you negotiate your "alone" space. Can you read a book without having the person disturb you or demand your full attention all the time? See how you handle giving your partner his or her space, too. All of these factors will help you learn whether or not you're compatible as a couple.

9. Have you experienced each other's individual lifestyles and found that they are compatible? Does one of you like to dress up in a tuxedo and go out to charity balls or high-profile parties at least twice a week—while the other would rather go to a movie or watch TV? Such differences may seem interesting or charming now, but eventually they may become a source of conflict.

10. Have you determined that your temperaments are basically the same, or at least compatible? If you've shared some of the experiences in this checklist, you probably have a pretty good idea about the compatibility of your respective temperaments. They don't have to be identical, but they should be compatible.

11. Are you certain you are falling in love with a real person and not an image? Many people fall in love with the *image* of a person. Men tend to fall in love with a woman's image because she's beautiful; she looks like their physical ideal of the perfect woman. Let's say a man falls for a woman with long blond hair, tan legs, and a terrific figure, but that intellectually, they're from different worlds: they have little in common except a physical attraction. Eventually he's going to learn to hate her.

If men tend to fall in love with a physical image, women often fall in love with prestige or power. Suppose a woman falls for a man because he's a doctor. He has a lucrative practice, is tremendously responsible in the community, and is held in high esteem. Her family and friends tell her, "My goodness, that's fantastic that you're dating a brain surgeon." But it turns out that he's cold and distant and emotionally unavailable to her. There is no way she can truly be happy in that relationship.

Don't fall for someone's image. You're not going to live with that person's image; you're going to live with the person's being, soul, values, and temperament.

Take your time with this conviction stage. Don't make the common mistake of marrying within a month or two of meeting. People who do this are almost always falling in love with the person's image (and with the sexual relationship), without truly knowing the human being they're going to have to live with.

FIVE PITFALLS TO WATCH OUT FOR

If it's beginning to seem that there's no end to warning notices here, that's simply because during the conviction stage of a relationship there are so many pitfalls. One reason is that this is the stage where there's an especially strong tendency to develop that "attachment to the outcome" we've talked about so much.

Even someone who wasn't terribly attached to any particular result earlier in the relationship may start feeling pressure now—from the partner, self, family, or even from society. Many people reason that if the relationship has lasted this long, there's only one option: commitment (which in our society usually means marriage). At this point, some people get almost desperate, determined to have that "happily-ever-after" ending no matter what.

As a result, we can make some pretty big mistakes during this phase. Let's look at five of the biggest errors.

1. ***We make a commitment before we become convinced that the person is really right for us.*** Otherwise known as putting the cart before the horse, this is a common mistake that can

sabotage even the most promising relationship. Either we move in together too quickly, a month or two after the relationship has started, or we marry too soon because—you guessed it—we've become attached to the outcome and haven't taken the time to really get to know the person. It's become so important to us to become part of a couple that we literally try to fit a square peg into a round hole. In other words, we have put commitment before conviction.

2. ***There's too much chemistry and not enough compatibility.*** We become blinded by lust. The sex is so good, we try to make the relationship work regardless of the compatibility component.
3. ***We turn a blind eye to the fact that this person has critical flaws.*** At some level we know our partner has critical flaws, but we ignore the flaws or decide we can deal with them. Refer to the list of critical flaws in chapter three. One of these flaws—alcoholism, anger, emotional unavailability, promiscuity, or any of the others—is a glaring sign that this person is *not* Mr. or Ms. Right. You cannot change somebody, and you do not want to spend a lifetime "dealing with" a person's critical flaws.
4. ***We ignore the fact that the two of us have fundamentally different value systems.*** Maybe your respective value systems do not equal a clear-cut case of "good" versus "bad"; they're just radically different. At any rate, there's a good chance that two people with markedly diverse value systems are two folks who will end up hating each other.
5. ***We ignore the fact that we have major lifestyle differences.*** If two people have drastically different ideas about what constitutes a happy life, there exists an abundant source of future conflict. If they can't negotiate and compromise on certain points, in order to build a lifestyle that's enjoyable for both, they will never have a future together. Ignoring the problems caused by major differences will not make those problems go away.

COMPATIBLE OR NOT? IT'S TIME TO GET SPECIFIC

"Compatible" is a very general term. You could say that compatibility is the sum of many parts. Examining all of the specific areas of compatibility will help you decide whether or not this truly is the person for you. It's very important for you to review these during the year or so that you're deciding whether or not to make a commitment.

Before we get into this list, however, I want to recommend a wonderful book by Barbara De Angelis, entitled, "*Are You the One for Me?*" I would suggest that everyone read this book during the conviction stage. It is very detailed and complex; it's great for analytical people. (You engineers out there are going to love it.) I found it valuable because it goes into every single possible detail to help you determine if a person is right for you.

Meanwhile, let's explore the questions I've prepared for you. If you answer them honestly, they will reveal whether you are "the ones" for each other.

1. Are you sexually compatible? I'm listing this one first—not just to get your attention, but because *if sex is important to you, and you're not compatible in this area, you will never be completely happy and content in this relationship.*

The first prerequisite to sexual compatibility is that the chemistry be there in the first place. You have to feel attracted to the person. That may seem self-evident, but you'd be surprised at how many people get into relationships that are lacking in passion. They think that, if the relationship has enough other qualities going for it, the sex part isn't that important.

I have a friend who got married when she was on the rebound from a long-term relationship. She loved the man she married but did not feel particularly attracted to him sexually. Although sex was very important to her, she married this man anyway because she felt that she could "get by" on love and companionship (and could tolerate lackluster sex). Well, needless to say, that marriage did not last. She says, "Being married to somebody for whom you don't feel that spark of passion is like being dead inside. For all practical purposes you do have to kill, or at least temporarily numb, a part of yourself in order to stay in a marriage like that. But sooner or later the 'real you' is going to emerge, and you're either going to go nuts, have an affair, or get a divorce." Fortunately my friend chose the latter option, and is now in a relationship that has plenty of love *and* chemistry.

Even if the two of you do feel passion for each other, there are other considerations about sexual compatibility. For example, how often do you like to have sex? *Different people like sex at different frequencies.* There is no "right" or "wrong" frequency, but it is much easier to be in a relationship with another person who is on the same basic "schedule" as you.

If your frequencies are just a little off sync, you should try to negotiate and compromise. Don't throw away a good thing just because one of you likes having sex three times a week and one prefers it four. You should also be aware that there are going to be variations in your individual sex drives at times. If you have a tough project at work and you're putting in a lot of overtime, or if you're ill or under emotional stress, you simply may not feel sexy at all. Your partner needs to understand that this is temporary, and he or she needs to be mature (and secure) enough to give you the emotional support you need. This maturity should, of course, work both ways, so that you offer your partner the same level of understanding you expect.

It's also important that the two of you have compatible *sexual styles*—that you're compatible in the ways you express yourself sexually. If one of you likes erotic talk during lovemaking and the other one considers this profanity, that's going to cause problems. But no matter how in sync you are, the genders *are* different (delightfully so!). In chapter four I described how most men are turned on by spontaneity, while most women like romantic ambience; make sure your love life has plenty of both of these elements. The two of you are individuals, and everybody has his or her own style. Good sex is a blending of two individuals who can express their sexuality in ways that make lovemaking a pleasure for them both.

Also, in a good relationship you become progressively *more* sexually compatible, which means the sex becomes better and better the longer the relationship lasts. It's a myth that sex has to become boring as time goes by. The better you know each other, the more you know how to please each other, and the more exciting sex can be.

2. ***Do you have compatible value systems?*** There's nothing worse than being in a relationship with someone who has a value system different from yours. If you are a person of integrity, free of the critical flaws we talked about in chapter three, you are not going to be happy with someone who lies, is unkind, or treats people in an abusive way.

Not only is your happiness at stake in such a relationship, but your own integrity could be at risk. The questionnaire in chapter four, about the criteria for getting sexually involved with someone, contained this question: "Is this a person you would want to become more like?" This point applies not just to sex but to overall compatibility. Never forget that if you're with somebody for any length of time you *are* going to become more like that person. The bottom line is, you don't want to be in a relationship with a person whose values you do not cherish.

3. ***Are your lifestyles alike, or at least compatible?*** There are several different lifestyle questions you need to answer. For instance, does one of you prefer to live in the country while the other prefers the city? This could be a problem. Does one of you long to live in a high-rise, while the other dreams of a house with a yard? Is one of you an early morning person, while the other doesn't want to get up before noon? Does one of you like to party all the time, while the other prefers to stay home and watch TV?

Of course there are going to be some differences between two people—that's where the concept of compromise comes in—but if you don't have some basic lifestyle symmetry, the relationship is not going to work. It may not be a problem, for instance, if one of you sleeps late and the other one doesn't. If, on the other hand, you both want to go to bed at the same time, and one of you prefers to stay up until one o'clock in the morning while the other needs to go to bed at ten o'clock, that is going to be a constant source of friction for you.

Lifestyles can also include children and even pets. If one of you has four kids who live with you and the other does not like children, that pretty much rules out the possibility of a happy relationship. If one of you has six cats and two dogs and the other one hates (or is terribly allergic to) animals, that could be a big problem too. No matter how attracted you are to this person, no matter how wonderful a human being the person may really be, if your lifestyles are completely incompatible you simply are not going to be happy living together.

4. Do you have some similar interests or some of the same hobbies? It's certainly not mandatory that you have *all* the same interests or *all* the same hobbies, but you have to have *some* activities that you enjoy doing together.

5. Do you have compatible financial styles? As with hobbies and interests, you do not need to have identical financial styles, particularly if you're a two-income family, which most families now are. But you do have to be in agreement about how you're going to negotiate money. If one of you is a spendthrift and the other is frugal to a fault, you're going to have some real conflict. Although this is a very sensitive area (it's number one on the "conflict list"), it is possible that you can compromise and balance each other, and reach some workable middle ground.

For example, the less conservative partner may encourage the other to try new experiences: taking trips, going to a fine restaurant occasionally, enjoying some of the real niceties of life. There's nothing wrong with that. On the other hand, few factors put more of a strain on a relationship than overspending. You cannot spend more money than you take in.

The two of you also must decide if you have similar financial *goals*. Are you saving money for a house, or for retirement? Please consider all of these issues carefully.

6. Do you have compatible intellectual styles? This does not mean that you need to have the same amount of education or be trained in the same field. One of you may be an engineer, the other a lawyer. One of you may be in sales or management and the other may be a blue-collar worker. The question is, do you have some of the same interests intellectually?

A good measure of intellectual compatibility is this: can you have satisfying conversations? You don't have to be interested in world affairs or literature or science. Even if all you want to talk about is sports, if you both can talk about sports and truly enjoy your conversations, that's fine. But if one is interested in world events and wants to have someone to talk to about that, and the other one prefers ESPN to CNN International, you may find eventually that you have no common ground, nothing that you can talk about. Eventually, you will grow bored with each other.

Intellectual stimulation is every bit as important as chemistry and passion. If one of you is much smarter than the other one, that can turn into a real problem, because the smarter one can come to feel as if she or he is parenting the other person, while the other person may feel condescended to. Resentment develops on both ends. It's much more stimulating to be with someone who's close to you on an intellectual level.

7. Do you have the same spiritual style? It's possible for two people to be spiritually compatible without sharing identical belief systems. There are many ways of being spiritual, and if two people differ with each other in the details, they can still have a happy union if, overall, they have the same spiritual style. I've seen relationships work very well even though the beliefs of the two people were quite diverse.

That's why the two of you do need to consider whether or not your belief systems can peacefully and happily coexist. While you don't need to have identical belief systems, it's important that you be compatible enough in this area that one of you will not feel hampered or criticized by the other because of a different belief system.

If one of you has a spiritual belief system and the other is absolutely resistant to any sort of spiritual framework, that could be very difficult on the relationship. I'm not saying that a relationship between a believer and an atheist is hopeless, but it can be very difficult for a person with a strong spiritual belief to be in a relationship with a person who has no interest in spiritual matters at all.

Even if you've decided your spiritual styles are compatible, you also need to agree, if you have or are considering children, on how you're going to rear your children spiritually.

8. Are your life goals compatible? For example, do you both want children? Does one of you want to retire now and travel the world, while the other wants to dedicate time, energy, and virtually all waking hours to building a business in the next five years? In that case you almost certainly won't be compatible.

We've talked about the importance of compromise, but the matters on which you compromise are the "small stuff" compared to some of the examples we've just listed. Compromise on the "big stuff" such as life goals can lead to resentment—very serious resentment.

Looking at this issue honestly can be tough because, if you decide that your life goals are truly incompatible, then the only loving thing to do is to end the relationship. Otherwise, you are compromising your happiness and that of the other person.

You can love a person–really love a person with your heart and soul–but this does not mean that you need to spend the rest of your life with that person. YOU CAN LET THE PERSON GO WITH LOVE. *You each have a life to live.*

9. Do you have similar personal growth styles? It is almost impossible for a person who is dedicated to personal growth to be happy in a relationship with someone who is not. How can you tell if someone is interested in personal growth? One obvious sign is that the person learns—from workshops, books, and the insights of friends and/or professionals—*and puts this learning into practice in his or her life* (as opposed to merely reciting theories and ideas). People who are committed to personal growth know they don't have all the answers, and they're willing to learn. They try to become conscious of their own blind spots and faults, and take responsibility for their own lives. They talk about mistakes they've made, without always putting the blame on someone else. People who are interested in personal growth are always open to learning, and they are always trying to become better people as well as better partners.

If you are a person who's dedicated to personal growth, you need a partner who is similarly dedicated in order for your relationship to be compatible.

10. Do you have compatible physical styles? What is important here is not that you have identical physical styles, but that the other person doesn't have one that offends you (and vice versa). If you're very health-conscious, it can be quite offensive to you to be with a partner who smokes. Not only do you feel that your partner is putting deadly chemicals into his or her own body, but that you are being exposed to these substances, as well.

You may be offended if you prefer somebody who is fit and you perceive that your partner is slouching. You may be disturbed because you genuinely love this person and want to be together for a long time, and you believe that the person's questionable health habits compromise his or her health and longevity. Or you may be frustrated because you'd like your partner to participate in some outdoor physical activity with you, but he or she would rather stay inside and watch TV. If your physical styles are just too different, you're probably setting yourself up for a lot of unhappiness.

By the same token, you need to honestly look at yourself and determine your true motives for being unhappy with this person's habits. Are you simply being too critical or controlling? Ask yourself, just how bad *are* the other person's habits? Remember that no one is going to be "perfect." Life is meant to be enjoyed, and moderation is a big key to enjoyment. People need their little moments of pleasure, without guilt.

As with other points on this list, if your styles are compatible, they don't have to be identical. What's important is that you share a basic philosophy of living. You don't have to do the very same exercise program, but you should have the same essential attitude, even if your attitude is that being a couch potato is the way to live. If you're *both* couch potatoes—hey, you're compatible.

11. Do you have compatible communication styles? Can you communicate your feelings to each other? This is so important. Some people are very analytical and they have trouble communicating with a person who is very emotional. We already start off with being male and female; that's enough of a difference to create some problems. But if you have compatible styles of communication, you'll be able to bridge gaps caused by fundamental differences.

Can you talk about and resolve conflict in your relationship? When your feelings are hurt, or you're angry with each other, can you express that and then get on with your lives?

12. Does this person consistently and frequently meet your needs? If you need to, refer again to the lists of men's needs and women's needs in chapter two. Do the two of you consistently meet each other's needs? If not, the relationship is not going to be fulfilling to either one of you.

You can only have a relationship that works if the two of you are compatible. The list just discussed—which I suggest you both review—will help you determine if there are any problem areas, so you can figure out if and how you can negotiate the problems and perhaps reach a compromise.

You may not be 100 percent compatible with your partner, but some items *are* negotiable. On the other hand, some are not. There are some realities you simply can't live with. Even if you love and are totally attracted to this person, he (or she) may not be the right person for you. It's better to find out now so you can both go on with your lives. Eventually you *will* find the right person.

WHEN CONFLICT REARS ITS UGLY HEAD

During the period of time that you're becoming convinced that this is (or isn't) the person for you, conflict is going to come up. You have to face the fact that you are going to have conflict with every person with whom you have any prolonged contact—and that includes yourself. There are six areas in which you're most likely to have conflict as a couple.

1. ***Money.*** Even couples who have compatible financial styles will at some point get into conflicts over money. If one of you loses your job, for example, times can get tough, and that can put a strain on even a good relationship. Even when times are good, money can be a sensitive topic. But if the two of you are financially compatible and are basically compatible in the other areas as well, you should be able to resolve your money conflicts.
2. ***Sex.*** If your relationship is built upon a solid foundation of mutual love, trust, and compatibility, you should be able to solve most conflicts over sex. If you need to, go back to chapter four, and review your own and your partner's sexual needs. In fact, you might try reviewing chapter four together; that just may open new lines of communication.
3. ***Accountability / Responsibility.*** I asked one couple I know the secret to their happy marriage, and the man said, "Well, we've had some rocky times, but one important lesson we've learned along the way is to stop blaming each other for our troubles." It's true that many couples have a tendency to point the finger of blame at one another—even, or especially, for trivial matters. People need to be accountable for their own actions, but they also need to realize that not everything that goes wrong is necessarily someone's "fault." Of course, there may be an occasional instance in which one partner truly is trying to escape accountability or truly is acting irresponsibly. Everyone lapses once in a while. If this is a way of life for that person, however, there may be a real compatibility problem.
4. ***Expectations.*** Even couples who are perfectly compatible can

sometimes have expectations that are out of sync with each other. If you've honestly examined the specific areas of compatibility talked about earlier in this chapter, you can minimize the chances of conflicts over expectations regarding major issues. However, conflict can still arise about day-to-day matters. Let's say you're both looking forward to a few days off together. One of you assumes this means spending those days watching TV and lounging around the house. The other assumes it means a few days of yard work and household repairs. Your different expectations could lead to a less than pleasant time off. You might be able to avoid a conflict altogether by talking about it in advance. In any case, the solution is to not view the situation as an issue of "right" versus "wrong," but to admit that the two of you had different expectations about how you were going to spend your time off. Then you can work toward a compromise.

5. ***Goals.*** Looking honestly at your areas of compatibility can ward off any serious problems here. But sometimes people's goals change over time. Or sometimes one person may seem to be supportive of the partner's goals in the beginning, but as time wears on the person becomes less supportive. At best there may be some compromise in order; at worst it could spell the end of the relationship. Regarding your short- and long-term goals, the two of you need to be as clear as possible—with yourselves and with each other.
6. ***Family and friends.*** If you don't like your mate's friends, or your mate doesn't like your family, that could be the sign of a serious compatibility issue. However, even under the best of circumstances, where everybody likes everybody else, conflict can arise. Let's say you're a woman whose husband's old college buddy has just moved into town, and you agree to let the buddy stay at your house for a few days until he can get situated. You like the guy, but then the days drag into weeks, until you wonder if he is ever going to find his own place. Your husband, on the other hand, sees nothing wrong with this extended stay. To him, it's almost like old times. Needless to say, this can cause a conflict. Or let's say both of your families have

been dropping hints that you should be starting a family of your own, whereas neither one of you wants children. In that case, it's the two of you "against" all of them, so at least you can present a united front—but there's a conflict nevertheless. Conflicts related to family and friends are very common; they're the stuff sitcoms are made of. In real life, communication and possibly compromise are called for in order to deal with these sometimes sensitive issues.

A good rule to follow is: *You should never marry, or make any other commitment to, a person with whom you have never had conflict.* If you've never had a fight or a disagreement, if you've never been angry with someone, you're not really close to that person. One (or both) of you is repressing your feelings. You're not being real with each other—and a relationship based on deception is almost certainly doomed to failure.

Even if you repress your anger (which amounts to pretending to be someone you're not) for however long it takes to convince someone to marry you, your true nature is going to come out eventually. You may one day explode in rage at your spouse, spilling out all the feelings you've been repressing for so long, taking the person completely by surprise. You may end up saying or doing something you will regret, something that will do irreparable damage to the relationship. This is not what either of you wants. This is not happiness.

Your next exercise is about resolving conflicts. It's another one of those long-term exercises which you are going to be doing over the next year or so. Use either the space provided in this book or as many pages as you need in your Relationship Journal. Whenever you have conflict on an issue during the next year, write down what the disagreement was about, and write down whether (1) you were able to resolve it, or (2) it has just become a constant replay, an issue that repeats itself over and over until it's a running theme in your relationship.

If you're honest and thorough, this exercise will teach you a lot about yourself and your partner.

Exercise 5-2. Charting Conflicts

List conflicts as they arise over the next year. Note whether you were able to resolve each conflict, and how.

Conflict	*Resolution*

IS IT LOVE . . . OR IS IT DEPENDENCY?

During the conviction stage of the relationship, when you're coming down to the wire on whether or not to make a commitment, it is particularly important to decide whether you are truly in love or just afraid of being alone. As in so many other matters, the answer to this question is rooted in your self-esteem.

The more positive your self-image is, the greater your ability to love.

Unfortunately, many people confuse love and dependency. Dependency means, *I need you in my life for financial support, or for emotional support, or because, for some reason, I don't think I can exist without you.*

Love, on the other hand, means, *I need you in my life because my life has more joy, more happiness, more light, more growth with you there.* A decision made from love is a real decision, based not on infatuation or passion, but on a true resolve to make that person as important to you as you are to yourself. If you love someone, that person's well-being and personal growth mean as much to you as your own. Love means really wanting what's right for someone else, even if what's right for that person means letting go of the relationship.

To make sure that you are not confusing love and dependency, your next exercise is a simple questionnaire to help you decide the basis of your own relationship. Answer on these pages or in your Relationship Journal.

♥ ♥ ♥ ♥ ♥ ♥ ♥ ♡ ♥ ♥ ♥ ♥ ♥

EXERCISE 5-3.

Janet's Simple Dependency Test

1. Do close friends tell you that your relationship is not good for you?

_____yes _____no

2. Do you create reasons for staying in the relationship that, when looked at objectively, do not balance out the negative aspects of the relationship?

_____yes _____no

3. Do you feel dread or even terror when you consider ending the relationship?

_____yes _____no

4. When you try to end the relationship, do you feel physical withdrawal symptoms that go away when you are both together again?

_____yes _____no

5. When you have ended the relationship, do you feel completely alone and lost in the world?

_____yes _____no

If you answered yes to any of the questions above, dependency may be a ruling factor in your relationship. If so, I would suggest that you are not ready to make a commitment to this person. You may want to go back to chapter one and begin at the beginning, by working on your self-confidence and renewing your commitment to *yourself.*

PUTTING IT DOWN ON PAPER

Let's say that your relationship is going along fine. You've navigated the switch, you've determined that you are truly compatible, you're confident that your relationship is based on mutual love and not dependency. As time goes on, you feel that you're really growing closer and that your intimacy is reaching a higher and higher level.

Even so, you still may not be ready to make a decision. You can take all of the compatibility quizzes and questionnaires in the world, do all of the exercises, and still not really know, in your heart, whether or not this person is "the one" for you.

Sometimes you really need a little inspiration. Why not get into the habit of documenting or recording your relationship? Not only can this be a delightful pastime, but when the time comes to really reflect on whether or not you want a commitment, you have tangible evidence of what this relationship has truly meant to you.

There are several ways to make a record of a relationship, and I imagine everybody who does so has his or her own favorite way. People who are visual, for example, might prefer snapshots. They may have scrapbooks full of pictures that make up little vignettes or entire visual histories of their lives. Some people are word-oriented; they write in their personal journals every day, they write love letters, and they save every love letter ever written to them. Some thrive on receiving or giving flowers or gifts. Some need to constantly say and hear the words, "I love you."

You probably know people who keep old love letters or greeting cards received from everyone they've ever known. Perhaps they read them at times when they're feeling down; it touches them and makes them feel warm and loved. You may want to take a cue from these people, and document the special times in your own relationship by sending cards or writing letters.

I suggest you keep a journal or diary, too, if you're not doing so already. Because your perspective can change even from day to day, the ability to look back on thoughts and feelings from a few months or a few years ago can add a sense of continuity to your life. I think scrapbooks or photo albums are terrific, too. If you take photographs of events that were fun—family outings, Christmas, vacation trips—looking at the photos can help you relive those wonderful times together.

How you preserve your memories is up to you; just do it.

By the way, even if some of those shared times are negative or crisis times, they are part of your history together. A time you spent in the hospital and were supported by someone you love can be very valuable in helping you decide what this relationship means to you.

You may be thinking, *Well, this all sounds like a pleasant diversion. But how can recording memories help me make a decision about commitment?* The answer is, it can take the edge off the fear that almost inevitably sets in when you start to make that decision. We're going to talk in much more detail about commitment in the next chapter. But for now I'll just say that when the big scary "C" word enters the picture, we sometimes forget all the wonderful things about the other person, and all we concentrate on are the negatives.

Having those albums, those cards, those tangible memories, keeps you from forgetting the good times you have had in the relationship. Seeing evidence of your love in a letter or a photograph, a dried flower arrangement or a poem scribbled spontaneously on a cocktail napkin, may very well prevent you from letting fear destroy your chances of happiness.

It is just as bad to leave someone you really should be with and regret it for years to come, as it is to stay with someone you shouldn't be with.

If all the criteria for a happy relationship are there, it doesn't make sense to leave someone. Yet this happens all the time. People let their fears take over, and they walk away from a wonderful relationship.

That's why I strongly believe that when it comes down to the stage where you want to make a commitment, having mementos of your shared history will help you focus on the joy of the relationship as well as your fears. And even if it turns out that the relationship does not last, you will be happy that you have something to help you look back on the time you had together.

To help you get started on recording your shared personal history, I'm going to give you a simple exercise to do.

♥ ♥ ♥ ♥ ♥ ♥ ♥ ♥ ♡ ♥ ♥ ♥ ♥

Exercise 5-4. Collecting Evidence

On this page or on pages in your Relationship Journal, note ways in which your partner expresses feelings for you, and you for your partner—such as gifts, special times together, occasional surprises, and other expressions of love.

Expressions of Love

The assignments for chapter five will continue over many months. Continue to work on deciding whether or not you're compatible with this person, and on determining whether or not you resolve conflict well. Review the checklists and questionnaires as often as you need to, alone and with your partner. In this way, you will gain many helpful insights that will assist you in the next step—the biggest "C" word of them all: *Commitment.*

♥ The Sixth Principle ♥

COMMITMENT

Commitment is an act of the heart: a decision from within to spend your life with another person. This is one of the most important decisions you will ever make, and some of the fears and doubts you felt during the conviction stage of the relationship may rise again and be even more intense. It's important to work through your fears so you can reach a decision that will make you happy.

And so here we are on the final chapter. It's been quite a journey, hasn't it? If, after all this time and all this work, you have become convinced that the person you're dating *is* the right one for you, you are now at a crossroad. You may be wondering if it's time to move on to a higher level, perhaps *the* highest level, of commitment with this person.

Let me pause a moment to clarify some terminology. Because society is changing to accommodate diverse lifestyles, the highest level of commitment for you may be different from the highest level for someone else. Your highest level may mean marriage, or it may mean moving in together, or it may mean exclusive dating. However, marriage is still the highest level of commitment for most people in our culture, so for the sake of consistency that will be my focus in this chapter. If the word "marriage" is not appropriate for you, substitute whatever word does work for you. The principles are the same no matter what.

This is because commitment is an internal act, an act of the heart. At its best, marriage is an external manifestation of that internal act, a pledge before God or a judge or a community. On the other hand, marriage can be just a way of going through the motions; *you can be married and not be committed.*

In essence, commitment is a stand that says, "I'm going to be there with you. You're the person I want." However you choose to express it to the world, when you have taken that stand, you have made the highest level of commitment you can make.

So now that you're giving serious thought to making a formalized commitment to your partner, what happens next? Once you've become convinced that this is the right person for you, do the warm fuzzy feelings take over? Do you feel all settled and content?

Is THIS the point where you finally get to live "happily ever after"?

Probably not. In fact, at this stage, when you really start to seriously consider commitment, you're more than likely going to be scared to death.

You've probably already dealt with the many fears and questions that came up during the year or so the two of you were "settling in" and coming to terms with being part of a couple. Presumably, you've worked your way through these fears. So why does this whole new round of fear set in, and why does the fear seem to be more intense than ever? The answer to that question can be summed up in three words:

Commitment equals Crisis.

The dictionary definition of *crisis* is, "a crucial stage at which future events are determined." With that sort of import, who wouldn't be scared? Fear is a highly appropriate response when you're trying to decide whether or not to make a serious commitment to a person.

REALITY CHECK . . . AND A CLOSER LOOK AT THE "GRIM" STATISTICS

I suppose there is something in all of us, no matter how experienced (or how jaded) we may become, that still wants to believe in "happily ever after." Most of us start out with that notion, though as we progress through life our idealism is usually tempered. If you're very young, however, you may still truly believe that once you find and marry the "right" person, happily-ever-after is a given.

What really happens is that when you get married you share your life's ups and downs, joys and sorrows with the person you marry. *And sometimes it doesn't work out.* Sometimes, no matter how right you may have seemed for each other, it ends in divorce. Does it seem I'm stating the obvious? Well, these truths may seem obvious to somebody who has been through a divorce or two, but may not be so apparent to a person who is young and romantic. It is not my intention to put a damper on anybody's romantic experience, but the truth is, divorce happens.

These days, anybody who considers marriage at all is going to be hit with The Statistic. We've all heard the grim numbers. "Fifty percent of all marriages," we're told, "end in divorce." And that percentage just keeps going up. That's enough to make anybody pause and think, "Well, maybe marriage really is a bad idea."

Let's try looking at this statistic another way. Even if 50 percent of marriages end in divorce, *I don't believe that all of those marriages were failures.* We think of them that way because society tells us to. But I don't think society's definitions of success and failure have kept up with the realities of our changing lives. Traditionally, marriage meant "till death do us part." Whether the marriage was based on love or not, it was for keeps. Perhaps this made sense for many millennia, when life was shorter and much of it was devoted to basic struggles for survival. But our lives are different today. We live longer, and most of us (in industrialized societies, anyway) expect more of life than just survival—we expect a measure of happiness and fulfillment.

We can safely assume, then, that some of those 50 percent of marriages that end in divorce do so because the two people have taken different paths. Of course, there are cases where one person wants to end the marriage and the other doesn't; but in the best cases, the divorce is a mutual agreement between two people who have loved each other for a long time and have taught each other everything they could. Haven't you ever met a wonderful couple who still support each other after they're divorced? They've gone on, they've found different mates, but they're still friends. Just because they are divorced, it doesn't necessarily mean that their marriage, and their commitment, were mistakes.

If you're a person who believes marriage is forever, no matter the circumstances, I would not expect you to agree with me on this point. But if you are willing to look at it another way, perhaps you will agree that of the marriages that ended in divorce not all were necessarily a failure. It wouldn't be unrealistic to surmise that, say, 25 percent of the marriages ending in divorce were actually a success by the standards we've just discussed. It's really how you look at it; either the glass is half full or half empty.

To further illustrate this point, let's take a look at the 50 percent of marriages we're assuming are a success because the couples are still married. I don't necessarily believe *that* definition of success is true either, because again, we're defining "success" by society's traditions, i.e., by the fact that a marriage has not ended in divorce. As we all know, however, many married couples are very unhappy. Perhaps they're staying in their marriages for the sake of the children, or in order to hold on to community property, or out of plain old inertia—but they are not each other's best friends, they're not committed, they're not happy. So, let's say, for the sake of argument, that 25 percent of the couples who are married *aren't* happy (some people might think that estimate is a little low, but I feel it's a realistic figure). At any rate, are those successful relationships?

I don't think so!

We could play with these statistics all day—the traditional statistics or mine (and I want to reiterate that my statistics are not official figures but are based on realistic estimates)—but in the end, no matter how we cut it we come down to this: 50 percent of marriages succeed and 50 percent fail (see diagram). Statistically you have a one-in-two chance of your own marriage working. The point here is to be aware of, but not ruled by, the numbers. After all, you and your partner are individuals, not merely statistics. You both have the power within you to make your marriage one of the 50 percent that really work.

HALF EMPTY. . . OR HALF FULL?

100% of All Marriages

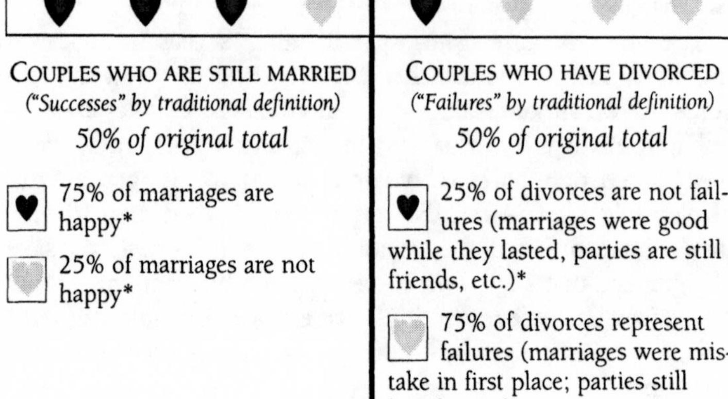

COUPLES WHO ARE STILL MARRIED
("Successes" by traditional definition)
50% of original total
75% of marriages are happy*
25% of marriages are not happy*
COUPLES WHO HAVE DIVORCED
("Failures" by traditional definition)
50% of original total
25% of divorces are not failures (marriages were good while they lasted, parties are still friends, etc.)*
75% of divorces represent failures (marriages were mistake in first place; parties still hostile, etc.)*

*Estimate by author

THERE ARE TWO WAYS OF LOOKING AT THESE STATISTICS BUT, EITHER WAY, THEY POINT TO A 50% SUCCESS RATE FOR MARRIAGE.

THE BIG TEST: IS THIS THE PERSON FOR YOU?

Let's assume you haven't been intimidated by statistics, and you're not letting your fears keep you from seriously thinking about committing to the person you're with. But you're still not certain if this person is "the one" for you, and you'd like to know if there's a way you can be more certain.

You've probably already guessed I have a questionnaire that will help you. This questionnaire, in fact, is your first exercise for this chapter. If you are thinking at all about making a commitment, it is very important that you do this exercise.

Take the questionnaire and sit down in a nice quiet place where you have solitude and tranquillity—perhaps a park or a garden, or just your living room with some peaceful music in the background. What's important is that you be alone so that you can concentrate on these questions and really reflect on each one.

Some of the questions will be familiar to you. The first few are from the list of questions you asked yourself in chapter four, before you had sex with the person. Some of the other points are from chapter five, when you were in the process of becoming convinced that you wanted to reach a higher level of commitment with the person. The reason for repeating these questions is that, presumably, time has elapsed since you answered them; ideally you have had at least a year to reflect. You know this person better now. Are your answers still the same?

As usual, you can use the space in this book, or jot down your answers and comments on a page or pages in your Relationship Journal.

♥ ♥ ♥ ♥ ♥ ♥ ♥ ♥ ♥ ♡ ♥ ♥ ♥

EXERCISE 6-1. THE COMMITMENT QUESTIONNAIRE

Answer these questions; consider each one carefully.

1. ***Is this a person you would want to become more like?***

   ____ yes ____ no

   If you share your life with this person, the two of you will become more alike. There's absolutely no question about that. Be sure this is someone you'd want to be more like.

2. ***Is this a person you would want your sibling, child, or parent to marry, if they were the same age?***

   ____ yes ____ no

   If this person isn't good enough for the other people you love, he or she is not good enough for you.

3. ***Is this a person whose company you could enjoy for an extended period of time without sex—for example, on a trip together?***

   ____ yes ____ no

If this is not a person whose companionship you truly enjoy, don't get married.

4. ***Is this a person you would want to have as a friend, if you knew you would never have a sexual relationship?***
 ____ yes ____ no
 This is related to the previous question. A big portion of marriage is devoted not to being a sex partner, but to being a best friend.
5. ***Is this person free of the critical flaws that we discussed in chapter three?***
 ____ yes ____ no
 You don't want to invest your time and emotions in a relationship with someone who has critical flaws. You will never change anybody for the better, but that person may very well change *you* for the worse. Don't risk it.
6. ***Is this person approximately your equal intellectually?***
 ____ yes ____ no
 If there's too great a disparity in your intellectual levels, it can lead to boredom, contempt, resentment—hardly bases for a happy relationship.
7. ***Is this person emotionally available to you?***
 ____ yes ____ no
 Does the person genuinely care about your growth as a person, supporting you when you need it? Or is it a one-sided relationship; do you find yourself always providing the support and receiving none in return? A relationship must be reciprocal in order to be successful.
8. ***Does this person really love you, to the extent that he or she could let you go, with love, if necessary?***
 ____ yes ____ no
 If it were in your own best interest not to commit to the relationship but to leave it, would the person let you go with love, and really wish you well? This is not to imply that there would be no period of grief or anger, but would there be genuine love behind that grief? When two people truly love each other, both people put their partner's needs, well-being, personal growth, and happiness on the same level of importance

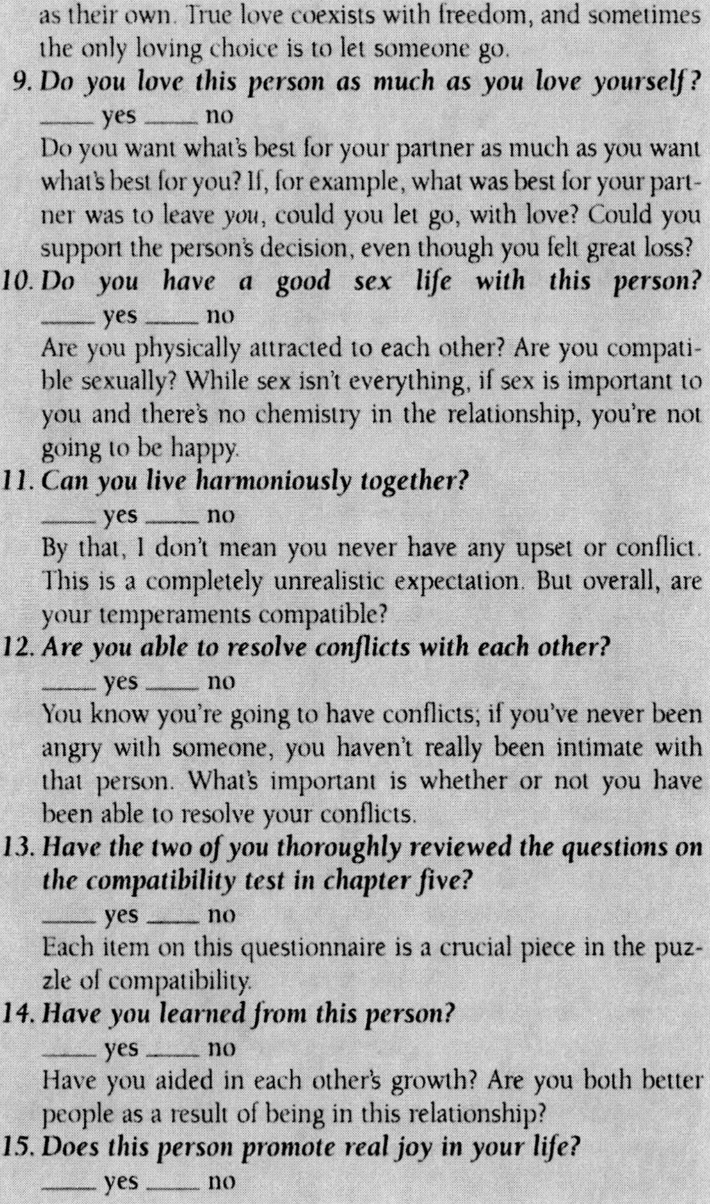

as their own. True love coexists with freedom, and sometimes the only loving choice is to let someone go.

9. ***Do you love this person as much as you love yourself?***
____ yes ____ no
Do you want what's best for your partner as much as you want what's best for you? If, for example, what was best for your partner was to leave *you*, could you let go, with love? Could you support the person's decision, even though you felt great loss?

10. ***Do you have a good sex life with this person?***
____ yes ____ no
Are you physically attracted to each other? Are you compatible sexually? While sex isn't everything, if sex is important to you and there's no chemistry in the relationship, you're not going to be happy.

11. ***Can you live harmoniously together?***
____ yes ____ no
By that, I don't mean you never have any upset or conflict. This is a completely unrealistic expectation. But overall, are your temperaments compatible?

12. ***Are you able to resolve conflicts with each other?***
____ yes ____ no
You know you're going to have conflicts; if you've never been angry with someone, you haven't really been intimate with that person. What's important is whether or not you have been able to resolve your conflicts.

13. ***Have the two of you thoroughly reviewed the questions on the compatibility test in chapter five?***
____ yes ____ no
Each item on this questionnaire is a crucial piece in the puzzle of compatibility.

14. ***Have you learned from this person?***
____ yes ____ no
Have you aided in each other's growth? Are you both better people as a result of being in this relationship?

15. ***Does this person promote real joy in your life?***
____ yes ____ no

Forget cheap thrills and gratification of superficial needs. Does this person help make your life truly joyful?

16. ***Does this person have a history of loving relationships?***

____ yes ____ no

Look at your partner's relationships with parents, siblings, friends, children, even ex-spouses or ex-lovers, if applicable. Do these relationships reflect a person who is capable of giving and receiving love, or someone who always leaves a trail of bitterness or rancor? You can gain much insight into somebody's character by paying attention to how that person interacts with other loved ones.

17. ***Does this person love you enough, and consider you compatible enough, to seriously contemplate spending a lifetime with you?***

____ yes ____ no

If your partner hasn't done so already, have him or her answer the compatibility questions in chapter five. Overall, your perceptions about your compatibility should be in sync with each other. Beyond the questionnaire, however, you really need to be sure that this person is giving as serious a consideration to a lifetime commitment as you are.

18. ***Can you drop all of your fears enough to visualize yourself living a happy life with this person?***

____ yes ____ no

It's possible you may still have fears—fear of being entrapped, of repeating bad experiences from the past, or of making a mistake. Or maybe you're worried about the changes the future may bring—what if she got fat, what if he became bald, what if one of us got ill and the other one had to assume responsibility for care? The mind is capable of conjuring so many possibilities. The question is, can you look beyond these, and if you can, if you simply let your fears melt away—*can you visualize yourself having a happy life with this person?*

19. ***Would this person support you in taking on new personal-growth or professional challenges?***

____ yes ____ no

If you wanted to take on an entirely new challenge in your life—change careers, retire early, work on your internal self instead of your professional self, how would this person react? If you wanted to do something that was totally different, would your significant other support you or critically judge you? Of course, it's impossible to be completely certain about how someone might react to a new interest you could possibly develop a decade down the road. You should, however, be able to get an idea of your partner's general attitude toward these changes. Pay attention to his or her reactions when you talk about your dreams. (And don't forget this works both ways; how supportive are you of your partner's dreams and goals?)

20. ***Is this a person that you now consider your best and most trusted friend?***

    ____ yes ____ no

    I know you've heard this so many times before—I've certainly been saying it enough!—but the greater part of marriage or any long-term relationship is being there for each other *as best friends.*

21. ***Is this a person you would want your child to be like?***

    ____ yes ____ no

    Think about this question whether or not you already have children, and whether or not you want to have children with this person. Very simply, does this person have the character traits that you would want to see passed on to the next generation?

22. ***Can you accept everything about this person, just the way he or she is?***

    ____ yes ____ no

    Truly accepting a person means accepting everything about that person—including previous history. Previous history may include an ex-spouse; if you're not comfortable with the relationship your intended has with his or her ex-spouse, you need to get this worked out. Previous history may also include children. I want to elaborate on this a little, because it's an issue that came up more than once with my dating-service clients. Some people (and not just men) seemed to have the attitude that their dates' children were "excess baggage." Of course, you don't want a person who has excess *emotional* baggage, but please know this: *a person's children are not emotional baggage; they're part of the person.* If you're going to marry someone, you have to love that person's children. You don't necessarily have to like the kids, but you have to accept them, you have to love them, and you have to make a real attempt to have a relationship with them. If you cannot do that, you are not going to be happy. (You must also accept it if the person has to pay child support; that is, after all, your partner's responsibility as a parent.)

If the person has custody of the children and those children are going to be living with you, there is no way you can have a happy relationship unless you accept them. Even if the person is not a custodial parent, and only sees the children once a month or once a year, you still have to accept them.

If you find yourself unable to accept everything about someone, it doesn't mean you don't love that person—it simply means that perhaps you're both better off separating.

23. *Do you have the same goals?*

____ yes ____ no

Does one of you want a child and one of you not? Does one of you want to see the world for a few years and the other want to settle down tomorrow in a small town, in a little house with a picket fence? If either one of you compromises your goals, the relationship is not going to be happy. If you truly want to take different roads, let each other go—with love.

♥ ♥ ♥

I realize that this has been a difficult test. There are very few people in your life to whom you will ever get close enough to consider marriage or any other form of profound commitment. More than likely, even fewer will actually pass this test with you. I have purposely made this a difficult test because you really do need to look long and hard at all of these areas. Life is full of uncertainties, and we can never predict the future with 100 percent accuracy. This does not mean, however, that we have to jump blindly into our futures. If we make wise and careful choices, using our heads as well as our hearts, we can greatly increase our chances of happiness.

If you do not completely pass this commitment test, if there are areas in which the relationship falls short, you have three choices.

1. ***You can continue with the relationship, and both of you can make a commitment to work on the weaknesses until you pass in all of the areas.*** If the problems are minor (and few in number), you may be able to turn the relationship into a truly compatible one.
2. ***You can plunge into a commitment without working on the weak areas of your relationship, rationalizing that the good will outweigh the bad.*** Needless to say, I don't recommend this option. If there are major problems at the outset, you ignore them at your peril. And even minor problems can turn into major ones if you don't work on them.
3. ***You can move on.*** If the relationship has too many problems, moving on may very well be the only wise and loving option.

If, on the other hand, the person does pass this test, asking him or her to leave your life may be a very big mistake. You may be letting your fears keep you from living the most fulfilling life you can.

In just a little while we're going to list some of the most common fears that can keep you from making a commitment. But for now let me just say this: if your fear is so great that you're considering ending the relationship, stop and think about what you're doing. Very few people will ever be able to pass this test with you, and if you've found someone who has, you have found a treasure.

THE TWO FACES OF RATIONALIZATION

When you're faced with a big decision that will have a profound effect on your life, it's tempting to resort to rationalization. It's only human nature to want to have plausible reasons to support our decisions. When we rationalize, however, we're usually not coming up with reasons so much as we are making excuses. I think most of us know in our hearts whether a decision is truly right or wrong for us; and if we inwardly know we've made an unwise decision, we can come up with some pretty elaborate rationalizations to keep ourselves from facing our folly.

There are two common reasons for people to rationalize when they're in the process of deciding whether or not they want to make a commitment to another:

1. If their relationship truly fails the commitment test, some people are so attached to the outcome—or, perhaps, attached to *attachment* (more on that in a moment)—that they try to rationalize away the failures, and go through with making the commitment.
2. If the relationship *passes* the commitment test, some people are nevertheless so afraid of making a commitment that they rationalize reasons for leaving the person. We'll discuss that in a moment, too.

ARE YOU ATTACHED TO ATTACHMENT?

Let's talk about the first common reason for rationalization. What if your relationship fails to meet many of the compatibility criteria, yet you try to rationalize these shortcomings in an effort to preserve the relationship? That's a pretty clear sign that you're too attached to the outcome. *In fact, you may also have an attachment to attachment itself.* It's possible that, in your need to be attached, you are choosing to overlook the possibility the relationship is all wrong for you.

The need for attachment is often manifested as an obsession with marriage. If you're thinking about getting married, are you clear on your motivations? That's what this next exercise is all about. It is a test to help you decide whether or not your own need for attachment is too great. As in previous exercises, please consider these questions carefully. Use the space in this book, or a page in your Relationship Journal.

♥ ♥ ♥ ♥ ♥ ♥ ♥ ♥ ♥ ♥ ♡ ♥ ♥

EXERCISE 6-2. ATTACHMENT QUESTIONNAIRE

1. ***Do you find yourself often fantasizing about your wedding or about being married?***
   ____ yes ____ no
   If you're a woman, you're more likely to be prone to wedding fantasies than if you're a man. In our culture women have been taught, since they were little girls, to dream about their weddings and visualize themselves as brides. Men, on the other hand, are more likely to become very attached, not to wedding imagery, but to some vague fantasy of domestic bliss. I have nothing against fantasies, but a happy relationship is based on much more than that.
2. ***Do you fantasize that every date is a potential marriage partner, or someone with whom you might have a child?***
   ____ yes ____ no
   This is a definite sign of attachment to marriage. It means you see the people you go out with, not as individuals, but merely as interchangeable parts of your fantasy. There's no way every person you have a date with could be a suitable marriage partner for you, or a good parent for your future children. There is no way that everyone you date can be compatible with you, based on the criteria in our compatibility questionnaire—and I hope you've decided that you don't want to be married to somebody who doesn't meet those criteria.

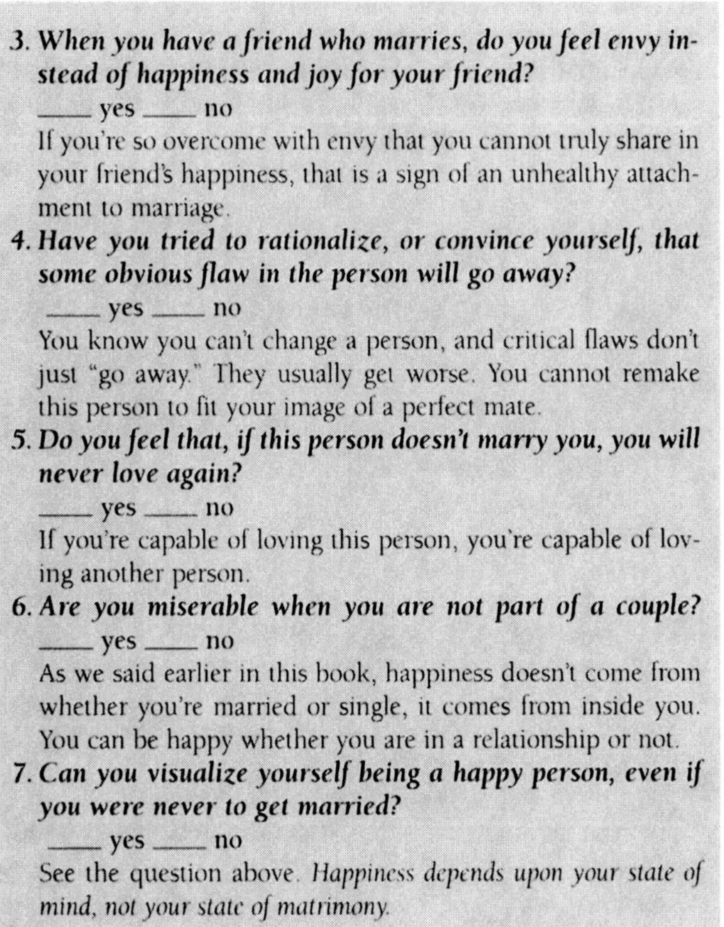

3. ***When you have a friend who marries, do you feel envy instead of happiness and joy for your friend?***
 ____ yes ____ no
 If you're so overcome with envy that you cannot truly share in your friend's happiness, that is a sign of an unhealthy attachment to marriage.
4. ***Have you tried to rationalize, or convince yourself, that some obvious flaw in the person will go away?***
 ____ yes ____ no
 You know you can't change a person, and critical flaws don't just "go away." They usually get worse. You cannot remake this person to fit your image of a perfect mate.
5. ***Do you feel that, if this person doesn't marry you, you will never love again?***
 ____ yes ____ no
 If you're capable of loving this person, you're capable of loving another person.
6. ***Are you miserable when you are not part of a couple?***
 ____ yes ____ no
 As we said earlier in this book, happiness doesn't come from whether you're married or single, it comes from inside you. You can be happy whether you are in a relationship or not.
7. ***Can you visualize yourself being a happy person, even if you were never to get married?***
 ____ yes ____ no
 See the question above. *Happiness depends upon your state of mind, not your state of matrimony.*

I hope you consider these questions very carefully. If you feel any of your answers reveal that you're more attached to being attached than you are to the actual person in your relationship, *get out of the relationship and do some serious work on yourself.* Don't get married, and don't get into another relationship, until you've developed a healthy relationship with yourself. You may need to do the work in chapter one again. You might even want to consider counseling or therapy. Please, please do what it takes to become a whole person, because if you're not a whole person, if you're not happy with yourself, *another person is not going to solve your problem.*

THE ELEVEN FEARS THAT CAN KEEP YOU FROM MAKING A COMMITMENT

Now it's time to talk about the second of the two common reasons for rationalization. Perhaps your relationship has *passed* in all the areas of compatibility, but you're thinking of ending it anyway. You're thinking of leaving this person. You may have worked up an elaborate rationalization for leaving, but more than likely, what's behind it all is fear. Here are some of the major fears that can keep you from making a commitment to someone who could be the right person for you:

1. ***Fear of the future.*** The prospect of making a commitment for "forever" can be very intimidating to some people. After all, who knows what the future may bring? It may be helpful to look at commitment in a different way. Rather than making a commitment based on a time frame, make one based on personal fulfillment and love. In other words, commit to the relationship for as long as it serves the personal growth of both partners: "for as long as you both shall love." This helps you to not worry so much about the future.

2. ***Fear of being hurt.*** Maybe you've been divorced or have broken up with someone, and have been very hurt. Or perhaps you haven't directly experienced this sort of hurt but have heard the horror stories from friends or loved ones, and you're just plain scared. Know this: *generally, it wasn't falling in love or making a commitment that caused the pain in these situations—it was making the commitment to the wrong person.*

3. ***Fear of choosing the wrong person.*** If you've both answered the compatibility questionnaire in chapter five (as well as

the commitment questionnaire in this chapter), and are both satisfied that your relationship "passes"—you're probably *not* choosing the wrong person.

4. Fear of becoming like your parents. This is an enormous fear for many people. Perhaps their parents' marriage ended in divorce. Or maybe their parents have stayed together, but over the decades the relationship has been dying by degrees.

To people who look upon their parents' less than joyful marriages as the model for matrimony, the equation is clear: commitment equals boredom, loss of freedom, drudgery, no fun, no sex. Marriage means two miserable coexisting roommates under the same roof.

If your relationship meets the compatibility criteria, however, this is very unlikely to happen to you. Remember, too, that you are not your parents. Think of it this way: you're two completely different people in a different time. Women and men now have more options. We have more freedom to write our own tickets. This means we have more power than our parents did to decide what sort of marriage we're going to create. We are not doomed to repeat our parents' mistakes, and we will not repeat them unless we choose to do so. The fear of becoming like our parents is common, but it really is not a legitimate fear.

5. Fear that there may be someone better "out there." Ah, yes, the grass is always greener on the other side. Traditionally men were the main followers of this belief, but nowadays women are just as likely to hold out for that "perfect person" who always seems to be just around the corner. If you're a person who subscribes to the grass-is-greener school of thought, you can easily become so distracted wondering about what *could* be that you completely overlook what *is*. You may look at your partner and think, "Well, this is a wonderful person whom I really love and who loves me. We have fun together. But what if we get married and then next week the *really* right person, the perfect person, comes along, but I'm already married to this person?"

I have a good friend who is not in a relationship now, and he's very unhappy. When I ran into him the other day, he said, "You know, Janet, I've waited for the perfect woman for so long, and I finally did meet her." Of course I asked, "So, Ken, what happened?" And he replied, "Well, unfortunately, she was looking for the perfect man."

My point is that there really are no "absolutely perfect" people—not in an objective sense, and not even in a subjective sense. There's no completely, absolutely perfect person for you. But if the person you're dating passes the tests I've given you, particularly the commitment questionnaire in this chapter, that person is extremely compatible with you on a very high level. You can share parts of yourself with many people in this world, but there are very few with whom you can truly share your life in a fulfilling way.

My advice, then, is not to worry about the grass being greener on the other side, and not to hold out for that mythical perfect person. Believe me, *the perfect person you're obsessing over will either (1) never arrive, or (2) arrive, but sooner or later do something to disillusion you.* If you have a good thing, stick with it!

6. Fear of making another mistake. This is sometimes related to fear number 2 on this list. If you've made a mistake in the past, if you've had a divorce or two, you may be gun-shy. You may have a tremendous fear of making another mistake. So you may decide you don't need to be married, and, perhaps, that you don't need to have anyone in your life. You give up. People often have a similar reaction when a business fails; they fail once and then they're afraid to get up and try again. But in love, as in business, you cannot possibly succeed if you don't ever take any risks.

7. Fear that the person will change for the worse (or the better). We've probably all worried about this at one time or another, in one way or another, but it's really just a form of narcissism. This concern can take two forms. First there's the worry that our partner might change for the worse. At some level, many of us feel we deserve a "perfect" mate who will make us proud. A man may worry, *what if she gets fat?* A woman may fret, *what if he gets bald?* Either way, it's a form of saying, *what if this* *person becomes a less than wonderful reflection on me?* That's pretty narcissistic, isn't it?

On the other hand, we may fear that the person could change for the better and that we'll somehow get left behind. Let's say a man is considering marrying a woman, and both of them are a little bit overweight. But she's just started a diet and exercise program. He may worry, *what if she loses weight and becomes so wildly attractive that other men start pursuing her?* Or perhaps a woman is worried about what will happen after her fiancé gets his advanced degree. She wonders, *what if he takes a good job and meets someone at work who has an equivalent level of education, and what if he becomes attracted to her?*

These worries can be little nitpicking concerns that bother us occasionally, or they can become obsessions. If they become obsessions, it's a reflection of our own insecurity. As for the possibility that our partner will change, that's one thing we can count on. Without question, everything and everyone changes. The trick is to take control of our own lives so that the changes we make in ourselves are always positive.

If we truly love our partner, we're not going to get upset if his hair thins or she gains a couple of pounds. And if we have a sense of security within ourselves, we won't be worried if our spouse changes for the better; in fact, we'll encourage those changes.

8. Fear of loss of freedom. Freedom and love coexist in a good relationship. Of course you're going to have to compromise on some matters, but in a healthy relationship you should not lose your freedom. A good supportive mate wants you to do what you need to do for personal growth and happiness.

9. Fear of compromise. Compromising on details is part of every good relationship. This does not mean you compromise your happiness or your ideals. It does mean that you meet the other person halfway in an effort to blend your lives. If you're truly too self-centered to compromise with another human being, you should live alone. *Don't torture another soul.* That's a sad and lonely option, and you'll be missing out on love—but if you are simply unable to compromise, it means you're probably not a loving person, and you really shouldn't marry.

10. Fear of losing out on fun. This is somewhat related to number 5. Eric was in a very happy relationship with a woman whom he was quite sure he wanted to marry. He and Elaine had wonderful sex, they had fun together, they took exciting trips. By his own admission, Eric was the happiest he'd ever been in his life. "And then," Eric told me, "all of a sudden this little voice started saying to me, 'Well, what happens if I get married? Maybe there's some single guy out there who's going to have more fun than me. If I get married, I'm going to miss out on that fun.'

"And then to make things worse," he continued, "a single friend of mine announced he was going to a Club Med. I guess I let my imagination run away with me. I imagined him arriving at Club Med, where there just happened to be an international convention of beautiful supermodels, and they all fell for him. I mean, I was torturing myself with visions of him in the midst of these gorgeous models, all fighting over him. Of course I was thinking, 'Well, if I were single and I were there, they wouldn't be fighting over *him*, they'd be fighting over *me*.' "

Fortunately Eric thought this through and came to the conclusion that his vision was pretty ludicrous. "After all, I know my buddy is just trying to get a good date," Eric said. "He even told me once that he'd sure like to find somebody like Elaine and settle down. This Club Med thing is just a diversion. He's really looking for the kind of relationship I already have."

Of course, men are not the only ones who fall prey to wild fantasies. Sharon is engaged to a wonderful man, but she went through a period of envying her single girlfriends. "It really came to a boil, I guess, when my friend Linda went to Paris," she said. "I was so envious. I began dwelling on the idea that she was going to meet this gorgeous Frenchman, who would take her to the Riviera on his yacht. He was going to buy her pearls and diamonds, court her and tell her how exquisite she was . . . then he'd buy her a villa, and the next thing I knew I'd be watching my girlfriend on *Lifestyles of the Rich and Famous*."

So what happened? "Oh, she had an okay time in Paris," Sharon said. "She even met a couple of Frenchmen. But they sure weren't the exotic men of my envious fantasies, and she didn't find herself on a yacht in the Riviera. Anyway, she returned home and now she's settled right back into her old routine of trying to find a date with whom she can carry on a conversation so that she doesn't fall asleep during dinner. She often tells me she wishes she could find a guy like my fiancé."

There's nothing wrong with fantasies, but if you let them rule your life, if you become obsessed with what you think you're missing out on, you may never learn to truly appreciate what you have. And if you envy your single friends, you might consider the possibility that they envy *you*.

11. Fear of wasting the other person's time because you can't make a commitment. Actually, this last point is an excellent indicator of whether or not you have a true fear of commitment, and, if so, whether it's an appropriate fear or an inappropriate fear. Let's say you're in a relationship with a person whom you genuinely love. It's the best relationship you've ever had, and in your heart you really don't believe you'll ever find a better person for you—and yet you want to end the relationship. Why? You feel you're wasting the person's time because you can't make a commitment.

This is a big red flag. It's somewhat like having a drinking problem; if you think you have a problem, you probably do. Similarly, if you think you have a fear of commitment, you probably do.

You might seriously consider seeking professional help to deal with this fear. I'm not trying to push therapy on anyone (and I'm not getting kickbacks from any therapists); I just feel that sometimes therapy is the best tool for dealing with deep-rooted fears.

Meanwhile, the key question to ask yourself is whether your fears are appropriate or inappropriate. That's what we're going to talk about next.

APPROPRIATE FEAR . . . OR COMMITMENT-PHOBIA?

While a fear of commitment is normal and quite appropriate, some people suffer from an inappropriate fear that is more accurately described as a phobic response. It is possible to have a phobic response to many things, including—strange as this may sound—to commitment. I wish to recommend an excellent book about fear: *He's Scared, She's Scared* by Steven Carter and Julia Sokol. Carter and Sokol address the different kinds of fears, including the phobic response to commitment. Reading this book can help you analyze your own fears and determine whether they're appropriate or inappropriate.

Let's talk a little about phobic responses. Peter, a regional sales manager for an electronics firm, survived an airplane crash. Even though he had previously been a frequent flyer he now found himself terrified of flying. While formerly he'd thought nothing of flying all around the country, now he could not bring himself to even board a plane.

This is a clear example of a phobic response. In Peter's case there was, at least, a traceable reason; his fear was based on something that actually happened to him. It was an understandable fear. Realistically, however, the odds were overwhelming that Peter would not be in another airplane crash. Therefore his fear, no matter how understandable, was inappropriate. Because his job required frequent flying, it could have been a very debilitating fear. Fortunately Peter entered desensitization therapy and is now regaining his confidence in air travel.

How does this apply to relationships? A person who has been through a bad marriage and bitter divorce may have been through the emotional equivalent of a plane crash. This person may be desperately afraid of going through that trauma again. Now, I could say that everything that applies to the airline passenger applies here, and that the odds are overwhelming that this person is not going to go through another bad marriage and divorce—but of course, that is up to him or her. (I didn't claim this was a perfect analogy, but it's a workable one.) The good news is that in a relationship, you actually have much more control over the outcome than the average airplane passenger has. So a person who has an inappropriate fear of commitment based on past mistakes very much has it in her or his power to avoid repeating those mistakes.

People may have an excessive fear of commitment based on bad past experiences, or on a general fear of the unknown. A fear of the unknown is natural, but if you let yourself be paralyzed by your fear you can miss out on some wonderful experiences. A few years back I went on a trip to Asia. I was excited, but I was also quite frightened: I was traveling alone, I wasn't on a booked tour, and just flying to Asia took nearly eighteen hours. I was even a little bit afraid of the airplane trip because once you're on, you can't get off. Once you've made that commitment, there's no turning back.

Once I got to Asia I couldn't leave well enough alone. I decided I wanted to go to Nepal, which, at that time, had been open to the rest of the world for only about twenty years. When I went to the airline and said I wanted to go to Nepal and travel back into the jungle, I was told, "Lady, if you go there and want to leave, you cannot turn around and come back. There is only one flight a week."

I'll never forget how genuinely frightened I was. But I thought about it and I ended up going anyway, despite my fears. And it was one of the most memorable trips of my life.

My mother has often said she wished she were like me, because I'm never afraid of anything. That's certainly not true; I'm afraid of many things. But there's nothing that scares me more than not living a full life, so I go ahead and do it. When I came back from my trip to Asia I had a tremendous sense of self-confidence and self-reliance. I had done something that many people would be afraid to do.

This lesson applies whether you're considering a trip to Nepal or a trip down the aisle. Don't let your fear of the unknown keep you from enjoying what could very well be the most rewarding adventure of your life.

What if you're not a commitment-phobe, but you think your partner may be? How can you tell for certain? Sometimes commitment-phobia is fairly obvious. Suppose you meet someone who's fifty years old, decidedly heterosexual, and reasonably attractive—but has never been married. This could be a clue that the person has a problem with commitment.

At times, however, it's more difficult to recognize commitment-phobia in a person, because the bare facts of that person's life may not reveal a problem. For example, the person may have been married before, and maybe the marriage even lasted a long time. But what sort of marriage was it? What if it really wasn't an intimate relationship? Maybe both people spent so much time at work that there was no real intimacy. Perhaps one or both people had affairs, which introduced enough distance that they really didn't feel committed to each other. *The fact that a person has a history of relationships does not necessarily rule out commitment-phobia.*

You should know that people who are commitment-phobes are great at rationalizing. Perhaps they've convinced themselves that they're self-reliant and don't need marriage. Or they have talked themselves into believing that they don't need a close relationship to be happy. However they've done it, they've developed a blind spot that keeps them from seeing that there's a problem area. If you're at all suspicious about the person you're with, or you're wondering whether you're a commitment-phobe, reading *He's Scared, She's Scared* (by Carter and Sokol) could be a very good investment of your time.

WHAT HAPPENS IF YOU TRY TO FORCE A COMMITMENT-PHOBE TO COMMIT?

When I was reviewing books on commitment, I found that almost all of the books have one of two messages. There is the "happily-ever-after" message, in which you do everything the book tells you to do and the commitment part just happens. You follow the steps in the book, get married, and live happily ever after. We already know it's almost never that easy.

Alternatively, there is the "how-to-nail-'em" message. These books tell you what to do if the person you want doesn't want you. I read about all sorts of strategies to manipulate a person into making a commitment.

If you learn nothing else about commitment, know this: ***you cannot make another person make a commitment.*** You may get another person to marry you, but as we've said before, *you can be married and not committed.* And while both people lose, the person who loses the most is the one who manipulates the other into marriage.

A commitment is an internal process, and for the relationship to really work, both people have to have undergone this process in their hearts, in their minds, and in their souls.

Let's look at what can happen when one person tries to force another to make a commitment. I'm going to tell you a story about two friends of mine, whom I'll call Jeff and Linda.

Linda loved Jeff passionately, and they had a volatile on-and-off relationship for many years. In his younger days, Jeff had been a very successful basketball player; he was a star in college, and then he played pro basketball. As is the case with many star athletes, Jeff had gone through a narcissistic stage where women were trophies to him. He even had a bet with one of his buddies about which one could sleep with the most women; it had to be a different woman every night for the most consecutive nights.

Jeff was a very good-looking man and, despite his Casanova tendencies, he was really a very nice person. But he was also a true commitment-phobe. Whenever he really started to like a woman, he would always bring someone else into the picture. He would begin dating another woman to give himself distance from the first. His favorite saying was, "Don't put all of your eggs in one basket."

Linda loved Jeff and wanted to marry him, but inwardly she felt he really wasn't good for her, because she was always unhappy. Unfortunately she couldn't bring herself to just walk away from him. She read all the books on how to catch a man—possibly some of the same strategy manuals I read—and she decided to make her move, literally. The tactic she chose was to move to another city—not really to start another life, but to try to manipulate Jeff into wanting her more. That didn't quite work. On holidays,

Jeff would go and visit Linda, but during the rest of the time he would date many women to maintain the emotional distance.

They kept up this long-distance, occasional relationship for quite a long time. Jeff still dated lots of women, but he always had Linda to fall back on. When he got lonely he could always go and see Linda. As a matter of fact he got lonely fairly frequently, because most of the women he dated were normal healthy people who, even though they liked him, would leave him once they learned what a commitment-phobe he was. A few of these women were actually much more appropriate for Jeff than Linda was, but they would leave because they were healthy people who were protecting themselves. They might consider being friends with him, but they wouldn't stay involved in an intimate relationship with him.

As the years went by Linda was still always there for Jeff. They might have gone on like this for years longer, but then something interesting happened. When Jeff turned forty, he was suddenly hit with a tremendous fear of spending the rest of his life alone. At the same time, he was going through a dry spell; it had been several months since he had dated anyone who really interested him. So he thought about it, and finally he proposed to Linda.

However, this was not your traditional, romantic, head-over-heels-in-love marriage proposal; it was more like a business proposal. There were conditions. Jeff proposed that Linda quit her job, move back into town, move in with him for a few months—and then if it worked out, they would get married. That's quite typical of commitment-phobics; they always try to hedge. They always try to leave an escape route.

Linda agreed, but she set a time limit.

As it turned out, they did get married. But happily ever after? No. Immediately after getting married, almost all commitment-phobes have a response of claustrophobia—and it hit Jeff hard. He felt trapped. He took up a lot of travel in his work to create physical distance, and he started having affairs to create emotional distance. He had sex with Linda less and less. In all ways, in fact, he was with her less and less.

Why didn't he just divorce her? Ironically enough, commitment-phobics also have problems committing to a decision like divorce.

This may be because what they really fear, underneath it all, is change. Or maybe they're just pathologically unable to follow through with anything. I don't know. I do feel certain that this is a couple who will probably never divorce unless *she* initiates it.

Let's stop and take a look at this. Linda got what she wanted. She got Jeff to marry her. That was what she had dreamed about for years; in fact, the whole process took over ten years. But Linda's idea of marriage was that, once they tied the knot, everything was automatically going to be okay. Jeff was going to find that marriage to her made him happy, he was going to make her happy, they were going to make love often, and they were going to live happily ever after. But did Linda really get what she wanted? No, she is very lonely now. She does not have the kind of relationship she wants. She's lonely because she's in a relationship with a person who is commitment-phobic, and if she stays with Jeff, she will never have the genuine intimacy and the true commitment she craves.

Take a lesson from Linda and Jeff. If you manipulate another person into a relationship, you will find yourself the loser. Never marry a person who doesn't genuinely want to marry you. Never manipulate someone into a relationship.

You only want to make an agreement to have a life with someone who wants to have a life with you.

POPPING THE QUESTION: HOW, WHEN, WHY

Now let's say you've taken the compatibility test, the commitment test, and all the other tests in this book; you've worked on your fears, and you have now become convinced that the person you are presently dating is the one to whom you want to make a commitment. In a perfect world, you would both arrive at the same place at the same time. At the same time you were making your decision about the other person, that person would be deciding the very same about you.

Unfortunately, as we've already pointed out, it's not a perfect world. The other person does not always arrive at the same place at the same time as you. So, what happens if that's the case? What happens if the words, *Will you marry me?* are in your heart (and, you hope, in your partner's), but nobody has said the words aloud yet?

If you're a woman, I would suggest that you wait for as long as you can and try to let *him* bring up the proposal. That may sound a little old-fashioned, but remember, there's still a bit of the traditionalist in most men, and you don't want to make a man feel as if he's being pushed into a corner. Waiting as long as you can generally means waiting until you start to feel resentment. Once you start to feel resentment, you have to address it. We've all heard stories of women who stay in a serious, mutually exclusive relationship with a man for years and years. There's no reason the couple can't or shouldn't get married; the man just never gets around to bringing it up. Or, if the woman tentatively broaches the subject, he manages to evade the issue. It's quite appropriate for a woman to feel resentful under these circumstances.

If you're a man who feels you're ready to propose, and you also feel the woman is giving you significant signs that *she's* ready, take the plunge. Go ahead and ask her. Tell her you want to have a commitment for life. You may find you were reading the signs wrong and she is not ready. There's no crisis; in fact, she will probably be flattered that you think so highly of her. If her response indicates fearfulness, however, you may need to backtrack a bit.

A FUNNY THING HAPPENED ON THE WAY TO THE ALTAR . . .

Sometimes when the possibility of marriage enters the picture, one person can suddenly become very critical. He or she may suddenly throw in some unreasonable conditions for tying the knot.

When Jake proposed to Francine, she told him, "Well, I would love to marry you, but I don't think we should get married until you're making more money." Jake asked her to define "more" and she replied, "I think it would be best if you made about twice as much as you're making now, so we can have a decent standard of living." Francine also let Jake know that she really wished he didn't have to pay child support. "It's going to make it tough for us to be able to afford a baby of our own," she told him. This was not quite the response Jake had hoped for when he took her out to their favorite restaurant and presented her with an engagement ring.

Marlene had a similarly unpleasant experience with her intended when the talk turned to marriage. Larry told her he'd really love to marry her, "but first I want you to lose twenty pounds, and I'd really like it if you got breast implants."

Unfortunately such stories are not all that uncommon. In any case, *a marriage proposal, or acceptance of same, should not be conditional.* It should be based on your total mutual acceptance of each other. If someone claims to want to marry you only if you drastically change your being, your solution is simple: don't marry this person. (Fortunately both Jake and Marlene made the right choice; they left their malcontent partners and eventually found truly loving relationships.)

If you're tempted to rationalize your partner's request, consider this: If the request is a true expression of that person's dissatisfaction, you're never going to be compatible. Or if the person is just stalling for time, he or she may be a commitment-phobe. Let's say you do lose the weight or increase your salary or make all of the changes your partner has requested. A person who is a commitment-phobe will find some other excuse to postpone the trip down the aisle.

Either way, this is not the person you should be marrying.

What if your partner says, "I'd like to get married, but I need more time?" If a person needs more time, grant it. I'm going to repeat the advice I gave earlier: give your partner as much time as you possibly can without letting real resentment build up inside you. If resentment starts to build, and your partner's stalling becomes a constant issue, this is only going to add to your feelings of insecurity and unhappiness. It may very well be that this person is a commitment-phobe. You can't change the person, so the only sensible choice is to move on.

By moving on, I don't mean you give an ultimatum. I mean you truly must move on. Remember Linda and Jeff's story. I don't believe in ultimatums, and I don't believe in strategy. Moving on means really letting go and living your life without the other person.

Perhaps you're in a relationship where you're happy and everything is going along fine. It's not broken and you don't want to fix it. It's quite easy, under these circumstances, to fall into a happy stalemate. *We're content,* you reason, *we love each other, so why should we go to the point of getting married or doing something that may change everything?*

There really isn't a problem unless your partner starts to feel resentment or insecurity and wants to have a more solid future with you. I have to warn you that this almost always happens to couples sooner or later, and these days it's not always the woman who pushes for marriage; often it's the man.

At any rate, if you are the one responsible for the stalemate and the other person wants a deeper commitment, you are going to have to make a decision. If, after facing the situation honestly, you find you cannot make a commitment, the only merciful thing to do is to let the other person go. While this may be very difficult to do, you do have to *truly let the person go* and not keep him or her dangling with any vague promises that you may have a change of heart in the future.

But what happens if, after a period of time, you are truly miserable and know you've made the wrong decision? Should you try to go back and make amends? Should you see if you can get the person to take you back? Maybe it's the romantic in me, but I say you should try. Keep in mind, however, that whatever problems the relationship had before are still probably going to be there. If you are truly a commitment-phobe and haven't worked on your commitment-phobia, you're probably going to keep repeating the same mistakes over and over.

BREAKING UP IS HARD TO DO . . . DON'T LET IT BECOME A HABIT

A break should be clean and honorable. You should never allow someone to go out of your life just as a tactic to getting the person back. It is a terrible maneuver, and it places you in the position of putting your life on hold. And, of course, there's the possibility that the person *may not come back*. When you let a person go, you must truly let go.

But let's say you *have* let your partner go, with love; you've made what you thought was a clean break, you've gone on with your life—and then the person does come back to you. You've probably heard the maxim that, if you set someone free and they come back to you, they truly belong to you. That may not necessarily be true. In any case, if the person you let go comes knocking on your door again, you have a big decision to make: do you choose to go on with your new life, or do you take your old love back?

You have to look deeply into yourself to find the answer to this one. Do you love this person enough to want to try again? If you truly love each other there is certainly a chance that you *can* go on and have a good life together. On the other hand, you need to consider the possibility that this person might leave you again. You really have to think about it. Is this a person who can't make a commitment? (Remember Jeff and Linda!) If your partner was unable to make a commitment to *stay* with you in the first place, there's a chance he or she has come back to you *because of an inability to make a commitment to* ***leave*** *you.*

If you take someone back, you may be setting yourself up for a pattern that could go on for years. I know another couple whose relationship almost makes Jeff and Linda's look like a match made in heaven. Will and Vanessa have been together for several years—well, in a manner of speaking. Vanessa just can't make up her mind about the relationship, and she has left Will again and again. She's left him for various reasons—for another man, or to take a job in another city, or just because she "wanted to be alone for a while." Each time she leaves, Will swears that will be the end of it, but he always welcomes her back. Vanessa has Will pegged as a soft touch, and she knows their relationship is a revolving door. She knows that when they break up, it will never be a clean break. She's confident that whenever she leaves him, for whatever reason, she'll always have a contingency plan. A few times she has had to beg Will to take her back, and once she even agreed to marry him (a resolve that lasted only until she'd moved back in with him), but these are minor inconveniences—a small price to pay for the knowledge that she'll always have good old Will to fall back on.

Don't set yourself up for a no-win situation like this.

Now, if your partner is truly commitment-phobic, there is the possibility that you may end up getting married but, at the first sign of difficulty, the person will be out of there again. Is this what you really want? Will you ever feel emotionally secure with such a partner?

There's one other possibility, however, when someone leaves you and comes back. This is a best-case scenario, the plot of many a romantic movie. It's possible that the person may only have been going through a period of uncertainty, and didn't really appreciate what the two of you had until it was gone. Maybe when your partner returns this time, it will be for keeps.

This is something only you can decide. If you let someone go and the person comes back to you, you must decide if you'll ever really feel emotionally secure with that person again.

The most obvious question to ask yourself is this: *During the course of the relationship, did the person leave you more than once for no real reason?* If you answer yes to this question, your partner may have a real problem with commitment and you'll probably never have peace.

THERE ARE LOTS OF GOOD REASONS NOT TO GET MARRIED—AND ONLY ONE GOOD REASON TO GET MARRIED

Many a commitment-phobe has tried to rationalize and deny the true nature of his or her fears by blithely stating, "I don't need marriage." Well, beyond the fact that those words can be directly translated to "I'm scared silly!", I would point out to our commitment-phobe that people shouldn't marry because of need, but because of love. It may sound as if I'm quibbling over semantics, but I'm not. If someone talks about "need" in this context, that person may be revealing a distorted view of what marriage is supposed to be about.

Never marry out of "need." If you cannot exist on your own, you should be alone until you can. You should be self-reliant and self-sufficient before you marry. Otherwise your marriage will be one of dependency rather than interdependency.

So many people get married for all the wrong reasons—lust, money, ego gratification, a need for attachment, or just because they feel marriage is expected of them. I will acknowledge that from a historical point of view, some of these reasons are not so out of line. After all, for most of human history the institution of marriage was more a business arrangement and a means of producing children than an avenue for personal fulfillment. But in the context of our society today, where happiness is a priority and relationships can be a means to happiness, there is only one legitimate reason to marry.

The only valid reason to marry is that you truly love a person: you are each other's best friend, your lives are better with each other than without each other, you want to grow with each other, you are the best possible life partners for each other.

If your relationship meets these requirements and you have made the decision to enter into marriage with your life partner, congratulations.

THE THREE ESSENTIAL ELEMENTS FOR A HAPPY RELATIONSHIP

We've just about come to the end of this book, but before we leave I want to give you one more little list to highlight, star, and remember. There are three elements a relationship needs to really work, and to really last:

1. ***Chemistry.*** It's a myth that chemistry goes away after you've been married for a while. Remember what we've said before: in a truly loving relationship, sex gets better and better as you grow closer.
2. ***Compatibility.*** Being in love isn't enough to make a relationship last; you must truly be compatible.
3. ***Commitment.*** Commitment means knowing you can count on each other to be there for as long as you serve each other's personal growth.

Those are the three truly essential elements for a successful relationship.

AND THEY LIVED HAPPILY EVER AFTER?

So now you've made the decision to become engaged, basing your decision, I hope, on the belief that the two of you are the best life partners for each other, and on the knowledge that your relationship is nurtured by a healthy supply of the essential elements: chemistry, compatibility, and commitment. *Now* is it time for "happily ever after"? Well, probably not. Probably you're going to be faced with even more stress.

As you may know, if you've gotten married before, or supported someone else through the process, the logistics of planning a wedding can pose a significant (though temporary) threat to your sanity. One or both of you may get a case of the pre-wedding jitters. You may find that, once again, your relationship is being put to a test, and that you're reliving every problem you've ever had in the past and a few new ones besides. But if you're in love and you're both truly committed, you will get through it.

Once you're married, and you've gone on the honeymoon and had a wonderful time, there's a period of adjustment. Most couples find that, even if they've lived together beforehand, there's something about marriage that shifts their perspective. Even in a jaded society, where so many people seem to slip in and out of marriages as casually as if they're changing clothes, for most people there is a finality about marriage that can be a source of dismay as well as reassurance.

You or your spouse (or both of you) may experience a little "buyer's remorse." You may have your first post-wedding disagreement, get the jitters all over again, and start thinking, "Have I made the right decision?" You will get through this stage, too, and I hope you'll be laughing about it over champagne when you celebrate your first anniversary.

So do you ever get to live happily ever after? In the books we read, in the romantic movies we flock to, there is little ambivalence about this. After the usual round of love and loss and reunion, the couple gets married, and there the story usually ends, with some variation of "and they lived happily ever after." Everyone adores a happy ending.

But real life does not exist within the confines of a two-hour movie or a four-hundred-page romance novel. Real life is full of uncertainties, but it is also full of possibilities. And I don't know about you, but to me that's the most exciting prospect of all. Who wants the tidy ending of a romantic novel when there's a whole exciting life to be built together? You have the tools to work with and the willingness to use them. Most of all, you have yourself and the special person with whom you have chosen to share your life.

How the story comes out is very much up to you. And you're off to a fine start if you realize that in real life,

Marriage is not an end . . .
it is a beginning.

PLEASE LET ME HEAR FROM YOU . . .

- ❑ If you are interested in information on having a private coaching session with me on the phone.
- ❑ If you would like information about volunteering to lead a Love Code support group in your area, or if you'd like to know if there is an existing local group.
- ❑ If you would like to share your story, or have questions, comments, or suggestions.

When sending your request for information on coaching or support groups, please include your address and a self-addressed stamped envelope. Also be sure to include your phone number, with the hours you can be reached. Address all correspondence to:

Janet O'Neal
O'Neal Enterprises
515 Post Oak Blvd.
Suite 500
Houston, TX 77027

Thank you for reading *Cracking the Love Code*. I'm looking forward to hearing from you.

Janet O'Neal

Printed in the United States
88305LV00002B/128/A